HAROLD S. KUSHNER

Conquering Fear

Harold S. Kushner is rabbi laureate of Temple Israel in Natick, Massachusetts, where he lives. His classic work, *When Bad Things Happen to Good People*, was an international bestseller. He was honored by the Christophers, a Roman Catholic organization, as one of the fifty people who have made the world a better place in the last half century, and by the national organization Religion in American Life as clergyman of the year in 1999.

Conquering Fear

HAROLD S. KUSHNER

Conquering Fear

Living Boldly in an Uncertain World

ANCHOR BOOKS

A Division of Random House, Inc.

New York

FIRST ANCHOR BOOKS EDITION, OCTOBER 2010

Copyright © 2009 by Harold S. Kushner

All rights reserved. Published in the United States by Anchor Books, a division of Random House, Inc., New York, and in Canada by Random House of Canada Limited, Toronto. Originally published in hardcover in the United States by Alfred A. Knopf, a division of Random House, Inc., New York, in 2009.

Anchor Books and colophon are registered trademarks of Random House, Inc.

The Library of Congress has cataloged the Knopf edition as follows:
Kushner, Harold S.
Conquering fear : living boldly in an uncertain world / Harold S. Kushner.
p. cm.
1. Fear. 2. Fear—Religious aspects. 3. Self-actualization
(Psychology) I. Title.
BF575F2K87 2009 152.4'6—dc22 2009013856

Anchor ISBN: 978-0-307-38589-5

Book design by M. Kristen Bearse

www.anchorbooks.com

Printed in the United States of America

For Ariel

What we choose, changes us.
What we love, transforms us.

JAN L. RICHARDSON

Courage is not the absence of fear but
the mastery of fear.

MARK TWAIN

CONTENTS

Contents

FIRST WORDS

This is my twelfth book. For all the others, I would start with an idea, present it to my publisher, and, if he liked it, proceed to write. For this one, my editor at Alfred A. Knopf, Jonathan Segal, came to me with an idea. He sensed that a lot of people were scared of a lot of things and it was draining the joy from their lives. Could I write a book that would help them? This book is the result of his suggestion; I hope it lives up to the vision he had.

In addition to Jonathan's astute guidance, I have benefited once again from the advice of my longtime editor, James H. Silberman, a revered name in the publishing industry, and the input of my agent and literary matchmaker, Peter Ginsberg of Curtis Brown Ltd. As in all my books, I am grateful to my wife, Suzette, for encouraging me when the writing was going well and for putting up with me when it was going less well. I have dedicated this book, a book about courage, to our daughter, Ariel, in tribute to the courage she has shown on so many occasions of her life.

I am constantly aware of what a privilege it is to have a book published in the expectation that thousands of people will read it and that their lives will be enhanced by it. I can think of few things in life more gratifying than the knowledge that my books have eased people's fears, assuaged their pain, and brightened their tomorrow. I remain deeply grateful to all of my readers for taking my words seriously and making my ideas part of their lives.

HAROLD S. KUSHNER
Natick, Massachusetts
October 2008

Conquering Fear

Conquering Fear

The Eleventh Commandment

DON'T BE AFRAID

> They shall sit every man under his vine and under his fig
> tree and none shall make them afraid.
>
> MICAH 4:4

Before I could write a book about what people today are afraid of and how they might deal with their fears, I had to write first about what frightens me. Only then would I be able to understand the fears of others. Fears can range from mild concern (Did I remember to turn off the oven?) to serious worry (She was due home at ten; it's midnight and she's not home yet!) to sheer panic (My brakes aren't working! The man has a knife!). I find myself worrying more about something happening to people I love than about something happening to me. I worry that they are vulnerable to serious illness, accidents, crime, natural disaster. To love someone is to make yourself a hostage to fortune, aware of all the terrible things that can happen to him or her. Whenever I read of a violent crime against a woman or child, a fatal automobile accident, a young person drowning, the rational side of my brain reassures me that it makes the news only because it is so rare, but my emotional side keeps saying, What if it had been someone close to me? (Even as parents fear for the well-being of their children, children's primal fear is that something will happen to one of their parents. I was once preparing a thirteen-year-old boy for his bar mitzvah ceremony, and I asked him if there was anything he was scared of. I was thinking of his performance at the synagogue service, but he spoke instead of his fear that one of his parents would die while he still needed him or her.) It startles me to realize that my grandson is only a few years away from being eligible for military service and might have to risk his life in a war. I worry about my grandchildren having to cope with the dangers and challenges of adolescence in a much more complicated world than either I or their mother grew up in. I worry about another attack on an American city, like the one on September 11, 2001, with heavy loss of life. I worry in the knowledge that I and the people around me can do everything right and still experience misfortune. We can be careful about what we eat and how much we exercise and still fall victim to a genetic time bomb hidden in our DNA. We can drive carefully and still be in the path of a careless driver. We can work hard at our jobs and save for our retirement, only to have events beyond our control force our employer to terminate our job or market events erode our savings. On those infrequent occasions when I have a bad dream, it is always the same one. I am trying to get somewhere where people are expecting me, and I can't get there. The dream speaks to my sense of helplessness in the face of forces I can't control and my fear of disappointing people who are counting on me.

I worry about losing those things that give meaning and pleasure to my life, the ability to read and to write, to give birth to another book or craft a meaningful sermon, the ability to follow the news and crack a joke about contemporary politics, the ability to recognize people I care about and remember where I know them from. In my rabbinic experience, I have seen too many people who were so sharp and insightful when I met them, only to have those qualities taken from them.

I worry about our planet becoming less livable, about our running out of places to live, water to drink, and even clean air to breathe. Sometimes I worry that I will live so long that I will come to see terrible things happening and be powerless to do anything about them, a war more fearsome than anything we have ever seen or an economic collapse even greater than the one we have just seen, one that will further erode people's savings, and sometimes I worry that I won't live long enough to see some things I look forward to. And most of all, I worry that all this worrying makes my life less enjoyable than it ought to be.

Columnist Liat Collins has written in *The Jerusalem Post*, "Perhaps deep down my greatest fear is that if I was to live in fear, I would never get anything done. You don't paint an apartment if you constantly worry about the imminence of earthquakes. You don't stay close to friends if you worry that they are about to be wiped out by war or disease. . . . If you acted on all the fears concerning children, you'd have to spend so much energy trying to protect them that you wouldn't have time to raise them."

How do I cope with all of these fears? Sometimes I do it by putting them in perspective as very unlikely to happen. Sometimes I find some small area over which I do have control—watching my diet, conserving energy, recycling more. Sometimes I simply do what most people do: I just stop thinking about unpleasant outcomes; sometimes I stubbornly believe as an act of faith that God has made a world in which tragedy is real but happy endings heavily outnumber tragic ones. I resolve not to let my fears of what *might* happen prevent me from anticipating with pleasure what I hope will happen.

Some years ago, a movie was made called *Defending Your Life* with Albert Brooks and Meryl Streep. The movie imagines people who die going to heaven, where they are put on trial to evaluate how they lived their lives. Every second of every person's life has been recorded on videotape, and in a heavenly tribunal, a prosecutor and a defense attorney summon up key moments of each person's life from childhood to his or her last days. The novel thesis of the movie is that the purpose of the trial is not to determine if one was virtuous or wicked but whether one had learned to conquer fear. That is seen as the goal of life. If in the course of a person's years, he or she never got over being afraid, then that person is sent back to earth to be reincarnated and given another chance to get it right. If people succeeded in overcoming the tendency to be fearful, they "graduate" to a more refined, and presumably more challenging, level of existence.

If overcoming fear is the first goal of life, the achievement that makes other achievements possible, we don't seem to be doing a very good job of it. People today are deeply frightened. Our lives are clouded over by real fears, exaggerated fears, and imaginary fears. At one level, of course, fear is a good thing. Our ancestors at the dawn of the human species could not have survived had they not been sensitive to danger. Whereas animals are born intuitively knowing what to be afraid of—a baby chick that has never seen a hawk will run for cover if a hawk-shaped shadow passes over it—human beings had to learn to know the difference between animals that could be approached and animals that had to be avoided, between the fire that would cook their meat and the fire that would burn down their shelters.

But as the world changed and grew more complex, it became more difficult to know what to be afraid of. It became harder to distinguish between realistic and unrealistic fears. Were we being prudent or paranoid if we didn't let our children play outdoors when we could not watch them? Should we stop going to movie theaters for fear of a flu epidemic, a terrorist bomb, or the prospect of being mugged in the parking lot? Is that foreign-looking man at the airport a dangerous alien or just someone on vacation? To make matters worse, local television news broadcasts eager to attract viewers and round-the-clock cable news channels desperate to fill their empty hours on days when nothing else is happening recycle every fire, every political scandal, every case of child abduction or food poisoning, to the point where people believe these occurrences are a lot more frequent than they really are. In the words of Dr. Marc Siegel, author of *False Alarm: The Truth About the Epidemic of Fear*, "Our infectious fears spread faster than any bacteria and ignite a sense of [imminent danger] that far eclipses the reality." Dr. Siegel goes on to say, "Anthrax is not contagious; fear of anthrax is."

Marketers and politicians have learned how much easier it is to manipulate people, to get them to do what you want them to, when they are frightened. In the next electoral campaign, take note of how much of what a candidate says is a promise of the good things he would do and how much is a warning of the terrible things that will happen if his opponent is elected. Margaret Miles, emeritus professor of historical theology, has written in the *Harvard Divinity Bulletin*, "Human beings have always had much to fear. . . . But humans have not always lived in societies in which fear was actively cultivated. . . . Isolated incidents are characterized as trends, and anecdotes are substituted for facts." She goes on to write, "Fear is hard on bodies. Anxiety is the number one health problem in the country, leading to epidemic depression, alcoholism, eating disorders, and prescription drug addiction. . . . American society is violent because it is so fearful." It would seem that we need to add unrealistic fears to the list of things we realistically need to be afraid of.

A recent article in the Science section of *The New York Times* reported that "worrying about terrorism could be taking a toll on the hearts of millions of Americans. . . . Researchers found that the people who were acutely stressed after the 9/11 attacks and continued to worry about terrorism—about 6 percent of the population—were at least three times more likely . . . [to develop] new heart problems." That represents more than ten million people nationally. If even a tiny fraction of 1 percent of those ten million were to suffer a fatal heart attack due to that stress, it would mean that more people will have died of fear than died on 9/11.

But how do we learn to overcome fear and live bravely in an admittedly dangerous world? Professor Miles suggests that we learn to "live with our uncertainties rather than cater to them." We need to rely on the ultimate livability of a world in which bad things can and do happen, but not nearly as often as we might think they do, and we need to know that, when we face our fears, we will not be facing them alone.

Dr. Gregory Berns wrote in *The New York Times:* "Workers' fear has generalized to their workplace and everything associated with work and money. We are caught in a spiral in which we are so scared of losing our jobs, or our savings, that fear overtakes our brains. . . . It makes it impossible to concentrate on anything but saving our skin. . . . Just when we need new ideas most, everyone is seized up in fear." What can we do about it? Dr. Berns goes on to suggest that "the first order of business . . . is to neutralize that system. This means not being a fearmonger . . . avoiding people who are overly pessimistic . . . tuning out media that fan emotional flames."

Some years ago, Gavin de Becker wrote a best-selling book called *The Gift of Fear*. His thesis was that we should be grateful for our innate sense that certain people and certain situations are dangerous, rather than brush off those intuitions as unpleasant. To live completely without fear is to live foolishly and dangerously. We would be emotionally blind and vulnerable to being harmed. But there is another sense in which fear can be a gift. Feeling scared reassures us that we are alive, that we are capable of feeling. Men especially have difficulty acknowledging what they are feeling. Therapists regularly find that when they ask a male client, "What are you feeling right now?" more often than not they will get a blank look in response or else an opinion, "I feel my wife is being very selfish," rather than an emotion, "I feel hurt and abandoned." Anger is perhaps the only emotion the average man can recognize in himself. Fear can break the ice jam and open us up to feel such emotions as hope, relief, and gratitude.

Adolescent boys, so concerned about being judged and evaluated by parents, teachers, and peers, so vulnerable to feelings of shame and embarrassment, are notorious for concealing their emotions. They feel safe only when they can put up a front of imperturbability—"I am a rock, nothing gets to me"—to the point where they may lose touch with the ability to feel at all. I think it's wonderful when a man or boy cries at the end of a sad book or movie (I often do). I take that as a sign of emotional openness. But at the same time, I recognize how hard the average adolescent boy works to avoid crying or to avoid anyone's noticing him cry. I have had dozens of boys tell me that they must be bad people because they loved their grandmother but didn't cry at her funeral. Too often, I read about a teenage boy dying in a driving or swimming accident because he had to prove to his friends (and to himself) that he wasn't afraid when any sensible person would have been. Maybe the occasional scary movie or ghost story around a campfire can be an experience in feeling scared and realizing that it is normal and nothing to be ashamed of.

Why, in fact, do people pay to watch scary movies? Why do we read thrillers in which the hero or heroine is in constant danger? Why do we enjoy tales of the uncanny and the supernatural? I think the answer in part is the reassuring feeling we come away with when the monster has been destroyed or the mad slasher has been brought to justice. We can then put the book down or leave the theater confirmed in our faith that life can be scary but order is restored in the end. Some years ago, I was flying from Boston to Los Angeles. When the plane landed, I had six pages left in the thriller I had taken along to read, and while the other passengers deplaned, I remained in my seat, unwilling to close the book until I knew that the hero (whom I had never heard of before I picked up the book and who was in any event a fictional character) survived his showdown with the villain. I can sympathize with the millions of readers who could hardly wait to find out whether Harry Potter would vanquish his archenemy, Lord Voldemort. Having been exposed to the reality of the power of evil (even if the characters in the book were not real), those readers needed to know that virtue would triumph. Their concerns (and mine) are not that different from those of the ancient Babylonians, whose New Year's festival featured a ceremonial battle between their god and the monster of chaos, a struggle whose outcome was as pre-determined as a professional wrestling match but nonetheless permitted the audience to face the new year with confidence.

In sum, a small dose of fear keeps us alert and alive, but an overdose can leave us perpetually tense, emotionally closed, and paralyzed to the point of inaction. If we could take a pill to banish fear, or if we could have a small part of our brain removed so that we would never feel afraid, it would be a serious mistake. Our goal should not be the total absence of fear but the mastery of fear, being the master of our emotions rather than their slave. Our goal should be to recognize legitimate fears, dismiss exaggerated fears, and not let fear keep us from doing the things we yearn to do.

Sometimes our unrealistic fears are nourished by too much information. But sometimes our fears are nourished by too little information. If we knew more about what was happening and what the true extent of the danger was, we might fear it less. We might be able to see ourselves and our circumstances more realistically.

Why are we afraid of things that in reality have little power to harm us? I have read of people who are so frightened by a thunder and lightning storm that they light a cigarette to calm their nerves. What are the chances of their being struck by lightning (assuming that they are indoors and not walking on a golf course wearing a suit of armor) compared to the harm they do themselves by smoking?

Professor Melvin Konner puts it this way: "We drink, we drive without our seat belts and light up another cigarette . . .

and then we cancel the trip to Europe on the one-in-a-million chance of an Arab terrorist attack."

I have read numerous articles meant to help parents deal with their children's fears. Many of them distinguish between realistic and unrealistic fears. To me, there are no unrealistic fears. If your young child is scared of monsters under his bed, the monsters may not be real, but the fear is real. There is something he is afraid of, and it takes the shape of imaginary monsters. The wise parent deals with those fears not by trying to persuade him that there are no such things as monsters but by leaving a night-light on in or just outside the bedroom so that the darkness is less than total. To a child, the world is an intimidating place filled with knives too sharp for him to play with and streets too dangerous for him to cross. It is a world of lurking dangers. No wonder he imagines the darkness to be populated by monsters. But introduce the tiniest bit of light into a dark room and as soon as the darkness is no longer total, its power to frighten is diminished.

My life as an author and lecturer, and the fact that our daughter and grandchildren until recently lived in another state, oblige me to get on an airplane several times a month. I know that bad things can happen on airplanes, but I set my not entirely unreasonable fears alongside my knowledge of how rare such incidents are and how statistically safe air travel is. In the light of those facts, I continue to fly, aware of my vulnerability but not intimidated by it, not paralyzed to the point of inaction.

(I once rushed to catch a flight from Atlanta to New York and found myself in the last seat in the last row of the plane, next to a well-dressed couple. We struck up a conversation, and they told me they were on their way to New York to attend a fund-raising dinner at the Waldorf-Astoria at which the guests of honor would be the king and queen of Thailand. I commented that I would expect most people on their way to dine with royalty to be seated in first class, not in the back of the coach section. The husband replied, "My wife is more comfortable in the last row. She's read about lots of planes that have crashed, but she's never read of a plane being rear-ended.")

But the light we turn to in an effort to dispel fear is more than just a quest for information. Since many of the fears that trouble us are irrational, they are not likely to be banished by rational considerations. I often suspect that when a person holds on to an irrational fear and cannot be talked out of it by citing facts, that fear is a cover for some other, deeper fear that he or she is unwilling or unable to put into words or afraid of having to do something about.

Some years ago, I met with a woman in my congregation who was terrified every time she went shopping with her young children. She had read a newspaper account of a child being kidnapped and murdered in a crowded mall. She had read a best-selling novel about a department store child snatching, and she was paralyzed with the fear that the same thing would happen to her family. I pointed out to her how statistically rare such crimes were. I reminded her that they make the news precisely because they are so rare and startling. She looked at me and said, "Rabbi, I know you're right. I've told myself the same things. But I'm still afraid. I know it's crazy. I know millions of people go shopping with young children every day and nothing happens, but that's how I feel and I can't help it." I recommended that she see a therapist, who discovered after two sessions that the woman was haunted by the idea that she was an inadequate mother. Her own mother was constantly criticizing her for the way she raised her children, blaming her every time one of them got sick or was injured. That was what planted the thought in her mind that she would not be able to keep her children safe in a crowd. Once the focus shifted from the fear of a kidnapping to her problem with a nagging mother, it didn't totally solve her problem, but it did free her to go shopping like a normal person. Shedding light on her anxiety made it seem more manageable and less frightening.

One of the components of fear that makes it such a destructive emotion is the sense of helplessness it engenders. We are sensitive to the difference between these two statements:

Something terrible is likely to happen.
Something terrible is likely to happen and there is nothing
   you can do about it.

The second statement is a lot more upsetting than the first. A sense of helplessness or powerlessness intensifies the fear, and people will do all sorts of things, rational or irrational, to lessen that sense. For example, whenever there is an airplane accident with significant loss of life, thousands of people who had planned to fly somewhere decide to drive there instead, despite the fact that the chances of being in a serious automobile accident are far higher than the chances of being in a plane crash. They do it because when you are a passenger in an airplane, you are close to helpless in an emergency. You have virtually no control over what happens. But in your own car, you have a sense of being in control. Similarly, some people diagnosed with a life-threatening illness will do almost anything—

travel to consult doctors in distant cities or foreign countries, experiment with bizarre diets—rather than stay home and follow the treatment recommended by their own physician. Doing something, however unproven or irrational, even something potentially harmful, is their way of saying that they are not giving up. They are taking charge of their own fate.

Because people rarely feel as totally out of control as when they are hospitalized, nurses have learned that patients will often feel less fearful and be more cooperative if they are given a measure, however small, of control over what happens to them. It may be something as trivial as asking, "Would you like your medications at eleven thirty or eleven forty-five?" or "Would you like to have the sleeping pill first or regular medication first?" But it helps.

Several years ago, I was hospitalized over the Fourth of July weekend with a severe leg infection that did not respond to even the most powerful antibiotics. The doctors, many of them recent medical school graduates who had begun their careers on July 1 and for whom I was one of their first patients, were stumped, and I in turn sensed their frustration, which did little to alleviate my own sense of helplessness as I lay there in pain. Accustomed as I was to being a person who solved other people's problems, it was frustrating to be told that there was nothing I could do to help myself get better. Anyone who has been hospitalized will remember those long nights and long stretches of daytime when nothing is happening, and how helpless, how utterly abandoned one feels at a time like that. Anyone whose ailment does not respond to treatment knows the haunting concern, Will I ever feel better? Things improved when they called in the hospital's top expert on infectious diseases, who ruled out the possibility that it was a deadly flesh-eating bacteria (mercifully, they had not told me they suspected that) and suggested what turned out to be the effective antibiotic. But my gratitude for his intervention coexists in my memory with the recollection of how helpless I felt while I was not getting better.

Prayer is one of the most familiar ways of alleviating the sense of helplessness. People pray in hospitals and doctors' offices, seeking a favorable test result or a good outcome after a treatment. On the weekend following the assassination of President Kennedy in 1963 and on the weekend following the attack on the Pentagon and the World Trade Center in 2001, churches and synagogues were filled to overflowing with people who didn't know what else to do with their anxiety and sense of helplessness except to turn to God. They needed to be able to bring their troubled minds and souls to God and ask Him for strength. And they needed to feel that they were doing something with their grief, their fear, their newfound sense of vulnerability rather than helplessly keeping those feelings inside them. More than anything, they needed not to be alone. It enabled clergymen of all faiths to give their people the message, Let us not panic and let us not despair. There is a story that on the eve of the Six-Day War in 1967, when Arab nations threatened to overrun and destroy the state of Israel, the head of a yeshiva, a college of Orthodox Talmudic study in Jerusalem, told his students, "This is a time of great danger. Don't just sit there doing nothing. Recite psalms."

Dr. Dean Hamer, in his book *The God Gene*, writes about a fishing boat off the coast of Italy in 1587 that was caught in a violent storm and was in danger of sinking. The captain, who had recently visited a chapel presided over by a monk named Francis, prayed to God and to Father Francis to save them.

The ship survived the storm, and ever since, St. Francis of Paolo has been the patron saint of travelers. Dr. Hamer acknowledges that we can never know for certain if it was prayer that saved the sailors, but prayer continues to be an attractive option for several reasons. First, stories of survival are told by survivors, so we are more likely to hear about cases in which prayers seem to have been answered than cases in which they were not. Second and more significant, praying can ease one's sense of helplessness. It can make us feel more hopeful and optimistic, possibly clearing our minds and freeing us to take effective action rather than remaining paralyzed by fear.

If the decision to pray or not to pray in times of danger were a results-based question, many fewer people would pray. So often, even when we pray with total conviction and sincerity, we don't get what we prayed for. One writer puts praying about a problem in the same category as worrying or complaining about it, a way of letting ourselves feel that we are doing something while in reality we are not affecting the outcome at all. I think that is too negative a judgment, rooted in his understanding of prayer as a form of begging, bargaining with God. I don't see prayer that way. When I pray, I don't think of myself as asking God to intervene and change things. I pray because invoking God's presence helps me to feel less alone.

A non-Jewish friend once asked me, "Harold, what do Jews pray for?" I answered, "Jewish prayer is less a matter of praying *for,* and more a matter of praying *with* and praying *to.*" As the theologian Martin Buber put it, when we pray, we don't ask God for anything. We ask God for God. We invite God into our lives, so that the actions we take will be guided by a sense of God's presence.

When I sit with a seriously ill patient in a hospital and pray with her, I explain that our prayer expresses our hopes for a favorable outcome. But more than that, I want the patient to know that she is ill not because God has rejected her or is punishing her for something. God is on *her* side, not on the side of the illness. God is sending her doctors and nurses, endowing them with skill and sensitivity. And even at night when the room is dark and deserted and she may feel desperately alone, she can call on God to keep her company. Asked by a television interviewer what I thought of an experiment that seemed to show that praying for people in hospitals made no difference, I told her, "God's job is not to make sick people healthy. That's the doctor's job. God's job is to make sick people brave."

Many religions urge people to give money to charity or to perform an act of generosity or communal service to accompany their prayers at a time of uncertainty and high anxiety. I would hope that neither the people who offer that advice nor the people who follow it believe that God can be so easily bribed. There is something else at work here. Years ago, my wife noticed that when I sat down to write in the morning, I would begin by writing a check to some charitable cause. At first, I told her it was just a matter of clearing a letter off my desk, but I came to realize that it was more than that. It was a kind of prayer that my writing go well, tapping into the generous, compassionate dimension I believe exists in each of us and hoping that my writing would reflect that. No matter how many books I have written or how well they have been received, whenever I begin a new book or a new chapter, I feel intimidated by that blank page in front of me. Do I really have something to say on this topic that people need to hear? In some way that defies rational explanation, making a charitable contribution helps me feel that much more confident about myself.

In much the same way, our biblical ancestors accompanied their prayers with a sacrifice, a lamb, a pigeon, even a cake of flour and oil if that was all they could afford, so that they could feel they were praying as generous people, not as selfish ones.

In a sense, all of our fears—fear of crime, fear of failure and rejection, fear of disaster—are all variations on one basic fear: We are not sure whether our planet is a friendly place, a world we can live in safely. Can we trust Nature? Can we trust other people? Can we trust our own bodies? As Dr. Gordon Livingston has written in his book *Too Soon Old*, "The primary goal of parenting, beyond keeping our children safe and loved, is to convey to them a sense that it is possible to be happy in an uncertain world, to give them hope." But before we can do that, we have to be able to believe it ourselves.

There are three strategies people employ for making a dangerous world seem less scary. Some individuals choose the route of denial, insisting that the world is totally just, that under God's providence nothing happens to people that they do not deserve. If those who hold this view read of a man being cheated in a business deal, they can tell themselves that he has only himself to blame for being too greedy or too gullible. If a woman is sexually assaulted, these people can comfort themselves by asserting that she was probably "asking for it" with the way she was dressed, the time of day or night when she was out, or the neighborhood she was walking in. If a city is severely damaged by flood or fire, they can say it is undoubtedly God's rendering righteous judgment on that city as He did to the wicked cities of Sodom and Gomorrah in the Bible. All those in denial can assure themselves that nothing comes into people's lives that they did not invite in. Good people have nothing to fear. If something bad does happen, those in denial can choose to believe that they did something to deserve it rather than that there is disorder or unfairness in God's world.

Sometimes people will call on the notion of karma, borrowed (and usually misunderstood) from Buddhist thought, to explain the misfortunes of ostensibly good people. When a child is born with a severe disability, his life impacted before he ever has the chance to live it well or badly, those who believe in karma can choose to tell themselves that his soul is being punished for its misdeeds in a previous life. I remember a store clerk who saw me with my young son, who suffered from a serious growth disorder, and said to me in all seriousness and in an effort to make sense of what he saw, "He must have been a very vain person in a previous life." Whenever I hear that line of reasoning, I am reminded of the comedian Sam Levenson, who would tell of how his mother went up to his teacher on the first day of school and said to her, "If my boy Sammy misbehaves, hit the kid next to him. He learns by example."

If someone's powers of denial are not strong enough to reconcile the harsh events of the world with the notion of a just God, he or she can go to the other extreme. Such individuals can see the world as a hopeless mess, contaminated by evil people and natural calamities, with no divine guardian to help. All people can do is arm themselves against the evil: trust no one; expect the worst; move into a gated community; look out for yourself and your family and advise others to do the same. The trouble with that approach is that human beings were not made to regard all other human beings as potential enemies. We need friends; we need to be able to trust people. Too much vigilance, too much suspicion poisons the soul and shortens our lives. I remember, as a former military chaplain, talking to infantry soldiers about the experience of "walking point," going ahead of the rest of your unit to check if any moving leaf conceals an enemy sniper, if any rock covers a land mine. One can do that for only so long, they told me, before it wears you down and you begin to see everyone and everything as a potential source of danger.

The late evolutionary biologist Stephen Jay Gould once proposed an alternative to Darwin's theory of "the survival of the fittest," the idea that Nature has arranged for the strongest and most ruthless to survive and the weakest members of any society to die out. He cited a Russian thinker, Petr Kropotkin, who suggested that Darwin, living in the teeming, congested metropolis of London, would have naturally thought in terms of the necessities of life being in short supply and people having to struggle to claim their share. But in the steppes of Russia, Kropotkin wrote, survival results not from competition but from cooperation, not from people against other people but from people together against the environment. Animals hunt in packs, and all share in what one has killed. Human beings pool their skills and resources so that each person benefits from things another can do that he finds difficult. The law of Nature, the law of God's natural world, is not the survival of the one who grabs more of life's good things for himself but the survival and prosperity of those who learn to share. Nature may contain a law of the survival of the fittest, yet it defines the fitness that leads to survival not by our readiness to compete but by our willingness to share.

Then there is a third alternative: not to insist that everything is God's righteous judgment and not to insist that everything is a dangerous mess in a world abandoned by God but to acknowledge that the world is a dangerous place and at the same time maintain the faith that God has planted in us the capacity to contend with those dangers and to overcome them. One of the central prayers of the Jewish High Holy Days, when we pray for a year of life and good fortune, enumerates all the terrible things that might happen to us in the coming year, events that must have been all too common for the average person a century or two ago: "Who shall live and who shall die, who by fire and who by drowning, who by weapon and who by wild animal." The prayer then concludes with the line "But prayer and righteous living can lessen the severity of the decree." That is, prayer and good deeds don't keep bad things from happening to you (though your charity and good deeds may keep them from happening to others), but they can make the bad things hurt less. They can lessen the *severity* of the misfortune, and that assurance may be enough to make the unknown future less frightening.

We distinguish between pain and suffering. Pain is the physical response to what happens to us; suffering is the emotional response, our becoming depressed or feeling hopeless, feeling like a victim because of the pain. As the saying goes, pain is inevitable; suffering is optional. Athletes, surgical patients, and women in childbirth experience severe pain, but if they are confident in their ability to deal with the pain and if they remain mindful of the reward waiting for them at the end of the pain, they need not suffer. Life will probably hurt us all, but if we can just remember that it may not be our choice whether or not to be hurt but it is always our choice whether or not to be afraid of the pain, it will probably hurt less.

More than eighty times in the Bible, God tells people not

to be afraid (usually translated as "fear not"). God says it to Abraham, to Isaac, to Jacob, to Moses. He repeats it four times in His first remarks to Joshua, lest Joshua be overwhelmed by the task of succeeding Moses. He tells each of the prophets not to be afraid of the demands of their role and commands them to tell the people not to be afraid as well. In the New Testament, Jesus repeatedly admonishes his disciples not to be afraid, and the angel's first words to Mary are "Do not be afraid."

Why do we need to be told "Don't be afraid" so often? I believe that God realizes how many things there are that frighten us, but He does not want us to live lives dominated by fear. Fearful people cannot be happy. Fearful people cannot be generous, charitable, or forgiving. Fear constricts the soul and keeps us from being as fully human as God would like us to be. In the Bible, virtually the first words spoken by a human being to God are an expression of fear. Responding to God's question, "Where are you?" Adam says, "I heard Your voice in the garden and I was afraid" (Genesis 3:10).

God spoke to the generation of Moses, the generation that left Egypt, and gave them the Ten Commandments, forbidding murder, theft, and adultery, enjoining them to respect the truth and honor their parents. But God also spoke to the generations before them and after them and gave them, and us, an Eleventh Commandment: Don't be afraid.

God commands us not to be afraid, not because there is nothing to fear but precisely because the world can be such a frightening place, and God realizes that we can never fulfill our potential as human beings if we are paralyzed by fear. Just as the bans on theft and adultery are not meant to deprive us of pleasure but to make sure that we do not miss out on what it can mean to be a human being in full exercise of our uniquely human gifts of empathy and self-control, just as the injunction to respect our parents is intended to make sure that we do not cut ourselves off from a major source of wisdom, guidance, and love, the Eleventh Commandment, the commandment not to be afraid, is meant to keep us from missing out on many of the blessings of life that are accessible only to those who are able to face their fears, see them clearly, and stare them down. Don't be afraid of being afraid. Our goal should never be the denial of fear but the mastery of fear, the refusal to let fear keep us from living fully and happily.

The Terror That Comes in the Darkness

THE FEAR OF TERRORISM

> You need not fear the terror that comes at night nor the
> arrow that flies by day.
>
> PSALM 91:5

Every member of my parents' generation remembered for the rest of their lives where they were and what they were doing on December 7, 1941, when they heard about the Japanese attack on Pearl Harbor. I and everyone my age remembers where we were on November 22, 1963, and heard the news of the assassination of John F. Kennedy. And we and our children remember where we were on September 11, 2001, when the World Trade Center in New York City and the Pentagon in Washington, D.C., were attacked. That morning, I was at Boston's Logan International Airport, sitting in an American Airlines jet, much like the one that was about to crash into the World Trade Center. I was waiting to fly to Toronto to begin the publicity tour for my new book when the pilot announced that our departure would be delayed briefly as there had been an incident in the air space over New York City. No one thought much of that announcement; delays in departure are not uncommon. Twenty minutes later, a second announcement told us to leave the aircraft and leave the terminal, as the airport would be shutting down. We left the plane and entered the departure lounge, where the television sets that usually broadcast the news had been turned off. At that point, none of us knew what had happened. Like virtually every other passenger, I turned on my cell phone and was about to call Toronto and tell them my flight had been canceled when my daughter reached me to make sure I was all right. She had known that I was flying out of Boston and that two planes out of Boston either had been hijacked or had crashed. It was from her that I learned what had happened. I found my way home in a daze, aware only that the United States had been attacked by an unidentified enemy. A beautiful fall day that was to have been the first day of a fulfilling experience for me was suddenly turned into a day of pain, confusion, and emotional turmoil. All I remember of that morning is the contrast between the perfect weather outdoors and the uncertainty inside my head.

September 11 changed everything and yet it changed nothing. We had known that such things happen before they happened to us. We had read newspapers and seen television accounts of terrorist attacks designed to maximize civilian casualties in Israel, in Northern Ireland, in African countries. We were all too familiar with the images of ambulances racing to the scene and of aid workers trying to separate the wounded from the dead, of politicians solemnly denouncing the crime. Why then do we see 9/11 as a day that changed the way we felt about the world, separating recent history into "before" and "after"?

St. Augustine, interpreting the biblical story of Adam and Eve in the Garden of Eden, explains how they should have known that eating the forbidden fruit was wrong even before they acquired a knowledge of good and evil. He suggests that Adam and Eve already had a *theoretical* knowledge of sin, of going against the will of God. That is, they knew that such a concept existed. But by eating the fruit of the Tree of Knowledge, they acquired an *experiential* knowledge of what it meant to sin. They now knew what it felt like.

In much the same way, before 9/11, we knew about terrorist attacks on civilian populations. But they always happened elsewhere. After 9/11, we lost that innocence. We now knew what it felt like to have our neighbors, our fellow citizens killed in cold blood by terrorist assassins. We had thought that we were invulnerable, protected by oceans to our east and west and friendly neighbors to our north and south. There had been wars involving American casualties, but not since the War of 1812 had Americans been killed on continental American soil by a foreign enemy. The events of 9/11 destroyed that sense of invulnerability. Novelist Deborah Eisenberg, in her book *Twilight of the Superheroes*, writes, "The planes struck, tearing through the curtain of that blue September morning, exposing the dark world that lay right behind it." And it is that dark world that we have been living in ever since.

After a decent interval when life shut down throughout America so that we could mourn and grieve, I resumed traveling to talk about my new book and inevitably, because I was known as the author of *When Bad Things Happen to Good People,* about the events of 9/11. People on the East Coast asked me if I thought that residents of the American heartland were as affected by the attack on New York and Washington as locals were. I found that New Yorkers felt it more personally. They had seen the smoke and found the ashes of the collapsed buildings on their windowsills. Residents of Boston, Connecticut, New York, New Jersey, and the Washington, D.C., area were more likely to have known someone on one of the planes or in one of the offices that had been destroyed. (I had served on the board of a charitable organization with one of the victims. The funeral for another was held in my synagogue.) But the reverberations of 9/11, the sudden sense of vulnerability, were felt nationwide. A man in Chicago said to me, "It could be my office building next time." A woman in Kansas City told me, "I don't feel safe going to a department store." As I write these lines several years after the event, we are still in the grip of that sense of vulnerability. On one anniversary of the attack, a woman wrote to *The Boston Globe*, "I miss the casualness of waking up and feeling safe. . . . I am beginning to forget what life was like before the terrorists attacked our country. . . . But I realize that what I miss most [is] September 10, 2001."

Terrorist math is simple. Kill one person, frighten a thousand. Kill a few thousand people, terrify an entire population. Terrorism has been defined as the effort "to create fear in a population disproportionate to the actual danger." The real targets of a terrorist attack are not only the immediate victims but all the people who will be sufficiently intimidated by that attack, to the point where they lose their nerve and change their behavior. You may remember how the D.C. sniper, one man with a rifle (aided by a teenage accomplice), nearly shut down an entire metropolitan area in Washington, D.C., Maryland, and Virginia by shooting people at random. People were reluctant to fill their cars with gas because several victims had been shot at filling stations. Terrorism works only when it causes people to say not just "something terrible has happened" but "something terrible has happened in a place my children and I often go to—office buildings, schools, a shopping mall. I'm not sure how I feel about going to those places anymore."

What would be a proper response to the threat of terrorism, one that does not deny the reality of the threat but does not let it succeed in breaking our will? Most of what has to be done to prevent future terrorist incidents will have to be done by governments, and there is not that much we can do to further their efforts, which would include better surveillance, prompt analysis and sharing of intelligence, and a readiness to negotiate coupled with the firmness not to make concessions that would only send a message to our enemies that terrorism works. But some of what has to be done to defeat international terrorism lies beyond the capacity of governments. Because the perpetrators of 9/11 and later incidents in Spain, England, Israel, and elsewhere were Muslim extremists, much of the hard work of uprooting terrorism will have to be done within Islam, not by Western societies confronting Islam, and there are some encouraging signs that moderate Muslims are trying to do that. Many Muslim organizations are condemning violence against innocent civilians and are working with Christians and Jews to dispel misconceptions and foster mutual respect and understanding. But there are important things that private citizens like you and me can do as well.

First and foremost, when we come to understand that the intended targets of a terrorist attack are not just the people they kill but the population they are seeking to intimidate, we will realize that, even if we cannot prevent every terrorist incident, we foil the terrorists when we refuse to be intimidated.

We can learn from the people of Northern Ireland, Colombia, Israel, and elsewhere that the best response to terrorism is to continue to lead our normal lives.

In the aftermath of 9/11, we have heard calls to keep on doing what we are accustomed to doing, because if we don't, "it will be a victory for terrorism." That mantra has been repeated so often that one magazine printed a cartoon of a child saying to his parents, "If you don't let me stay up to watch *American Idol*, then the terrorists will have won." Nonetheless, the advice is correct. The first and best response to terrorism is not to let our enemies scare us out of doing what we want to do. If they hijack airplanes, we must continue to get on airplanes. If they bomb a subway or a coffee shop, we must continue to ride the subways and patronize the coffee shops. It may be hard to summon up the courage to do these things, but if we don't, we hand our world over to the forces of violence. People do even more difficult things every day. An Israeli man whose daughter had been badly burned in the bombing of a school bus was quoted as saying, "There are worse things than dying, and one of them is to live every hour of every day of your life in fear. We are not going to do that." A Colombian businessman explained why he continued to go to his office every day, even though it meant leaving his home at a different time, in a different car, by a different route every morning and hiring bodyguards to follow him in a second vehicle: "I've invested my whole life in that business. If I let the criminals scare me away from going to work, I let them rob me of my life." Many of us of a certain age remember with admiration the steadfastness of Londoners during the Nazi blitz in World War II. London was bombed every night. Buildings were destroyed, and people were killed. But Londoners huddled in their shelters overnight, and in the morning life went on.

The power of a terrorist act, the secret of its effectiveness, lies in its randomness. If any bus, any coffee shop can be the target of a suicide bomber, then no bus, no coffee shop is safe, and so one could argue, we should avoid them all. But in that randomness may lie the ultimate weakness of terrorist intimidation and the key to defeating it. The terrorist wants you to think, If any shopping mall can be a target, then no shopping mall can be guaranteed safe. But why can't we think instead, If there are a hundred thousand shopping malls in America, even if today is the day a terrorist cell plans to bomb a shopping mall, the odds are a hundred thousand to one against its being the one I'm going to. Statistically, I'm in more danger from other drivers on the way to the mall than I am from a terrorist bomb once I get there.

If terrorists succeed in killing dozens, even hundreds of victims but do not cause the targeted population as a whole to live in fear, they will have failed. Mariane Pearl, whose husband, *Wall Street Journal* reporter Daniel Pearl, was abducted and murdered by Muslim fanatics, told an interviewer, "Terrorism is a psychological weapon. It stops you from claiming the world as your own. It stops you from relating to other people. It creates fear and hatred. The only way to fight terrorism as a citizen is to deny them those emotions. . . . The one thing they are not expecting is my happiness. That is true revenge."

Until the day comes when governments and religious authorities work to marginalize the aspiring terrorist, we may have to learn to live with the danger of terrorism the way we have learned to live with the dangers of drunk drivers, urban crime, and exploding gas lines. When these things happen, they are indisputably tragic, causing innocent victims to suffer and their families to grieve, but life goes on.

In time, I believe, we will learn to cope with international terror the way we have learned to cope with serial killers and identity theft, by responding with prudence rather than panic. We minimize the danger of being mugged by avoiding certain neighborhoods, not going out alone at night if we can help it, and being willing to pay taxes to maintain an adequate police force. And even then, we can do everything right and still be a victim. One can be a victim anywhere. But that knowledge does not scare us away from going shopping or to the movies. It is one of the tragedies of life that in every population a certain number of individuals will be violent criminals, abusers, and swindlers. But it would be a greater tragedy if that fact kept us from enjoying life and taught us to regard everyone with suspicion. Similarly, in an age of terrorist threats, we put up with taking our shoes off at the airport and opening the trunks of our cars when we enter a high-rise garage. Israelis years ago became used to having their bags and purses searched when they enter a department store. In these cases, we have chosen to be vigilant but not intimidated.

One of my favorite writers, Dr. Gordon Livingston, in his book *And Never Stop Dancing*, shares a story told to him by a patient. In 2003, with memories of 9/11 fresh in many people's minds, his patient was attending a concert of the Baltimore Symphony Orchestra. At one point, the lights in the hall went out. Many people wondered if Baltimore had been attacked. But *"the orchestra kept playing.* Sitting in the dark, unable to see the conductor or their scores, the musicians played on flawlessly. . . . The ovation at the end of the piece [was] especially heartfelt." We too, in a time when darkness threatens to envelop us, can do nothing more helpful or more courageous than to ignore the darkness and go on playing.

The attacks on New York and Washington on 9/11 changed the calculus about dealing with terrorists in another way. There had been instances of people hijacking airliners before 9/11, to or from Cuba or in the Middle East, to make a political statement. The standard response was to preserve lives at any cost. Let them have the plane; let them land it safely somewhere, anywhere, and then we will negotiate, or we will pressure the host country to arrest them. The assumption was that the hijackers had every reason to want to survive, if only to be able to broadcast their grievances to the world. September 11 introduced a new element. The perpetrators were not interested in being heard or making a statement. They wanted to hurt the United States as badly as possible, even if it meant dying in the act. What made the difference? The principal motivation providing the energy for what they did was no longer political but religious, and that is bad news. People can compromise on political disagreements, but how do you compromise on matters of faith? As long as the conflict in Northern Ireland is about economic inequality and sharing political power, people of goodwill should be able to work something out. But if the dispute one day devolves into a quarrel over the merits of Protestant and Catholic Christianity, how will they ever agree? If the conflict in the Middle East can be confined to where to draw the border between a Jewish state and a Palestinian state, I can imagine people reaching an agreement. But when you have one side brandishing biblical passages about God promising the land to their group and the other side citing the Koran to insist that any territory once controlled by Islam, including not only Israel but Spain and much of Europe and Africa, can never be alienated from Muslim rule, there will be little room for agreement.

Terrorism fueled by religious fanaticism represents a more difficult challenge to Western democracies in part because Western democracies tend to be committed to the free exercise of speech and religion, and their legal representatives are reluctant to take action against mosques that preach jihad or churches that celebrate the bombing of abortion clinics. The effort to dampen the fires of fanaticism will have to come from within the religions themselves. Any religion that aspires to be taken seriously in the twenty-first century will have to proclaim loudly and unequivocally that violence in the name of God is a sin and an act of blasphemy. They will have to explain the bloodshed in the Bible, in the Crusades, and in the formative years of Islam as a relic of a time when people had not yet come to understand that God abhors the murder of the innocent.

The Bible tells us that when King Solomon built the Temple in Jerusalem, "only finished stones cut at a quarry were used, so that no hammer or ax or any iron tool was heard in the Temple while it was being built" (1 Kings 6:7). For Solomon, whose name means "man of peace," the Temple would be a sanctuary undefiled by the implements that were so often turned into weapons. Violence may sometimes be necessary, but it can never truly be good. It is always a concession to human weakness. Most world religions would like to believe that living in peace is the natural condition of human beings, and conflict arises only as a result of mistakes or bad choices. But some students of human nature have come to suspect that this outlook is more ideal than reality, that conflict is normal and peace is the exception, born of great effort. They see the testosterone-fueled drive of men to keep what they have and even augment it as a survival aid in primitive times, one that we have not outgrown. Philosopher-psychologist William James, in his classic essay "The Moral Equivalent of War," expresses his concern that young men will always be attracted to war as a way of proving their strength and courage to themselves and to others, and he urges society to find a less destructive way of letting them do that. A rabbinic legend imagines Cain and Abel quarreling over who will get the choicest land and the most desirable women, the quarrel ending with Cain killing his brother. I worry about the human condition when in a history of the American Civil War, I read the description of crowds of spectators bringing their picnic baskets to watch the bloody battle of Antietam, and of soldiers singing and whistling as they march off to war as if it were a football game. It frightens me when I see how readily people resort to violence whenever they are frustrated or mistreated, and I often find myself wishing that more religious leaders would be as outspoken in urging people to sublimate their taste for violence as they are in urging them to control their sex drives.

Nations have to defend themselves against enemies. Winning war is often a matter of national life or death, which is why we tend to confer the appellation "the Great" to rulers who have won wars more often than to those who have presided over periods of economic prosperity. Societies have to pursue and punish criminals. But a people must always remember that violence should be a departure from its authentic way of life, not an expression of it. That is why Solomon tried to keep his Temple, the House of God, a refuge from the clash of arms and the exercise of iron weapons. When I was an army chaplain, my Christian colleagues and I spent many hours debating the question of whether it was appropriate for soldiers on duty to bring their weapons into the chapel. Would that represent compromising the holiness of the sanctuary, or would it be a case of their dedicating their arms to the service of God?

In all of my years as a student and teacher of the Bible, no passage has perplexed me more than chapter 22 of Genesis, the passage we refer to as the Binding of Isaac. God tells Abraham to take his beloved son Isaac, born to him after years of yearning, and offer him up as a sacrifice. Abraham binds his son on an altar and is about to kill him when God speaks to him a second time, telling him to spare the boy's life. (The rock at the heart of Jerusalem's Dome of the Rock is reputed to be the rock on which Isaac was bound. I visited the Dome of the Rock years ago, when it was accessible to tourists, and I can believe the tradition. Rarely has an inanimate object radiated such a sense of mystical presence, what some cultures call mana.)

Reading that story every year, I never knew whom to be more disappointed in, God for making such a demand or Abraham for so unhesitatingly agreeing to it. I could not accept Kierkegaard's interpretation, anticipated by any number of rabbinic commentators, that God's command must supersede our own sense of morality. I would ask myself, Where does my sense of morality, my innate sense that murder is wrong, come from if not from God?

Then, a few years ago, I finally came up with an interpretation of Genesis 22 that I can live with. The biblical narrative describes the episode as a test: "It came to pass after those events that the Lord tested Abraham" (Genesis 22:1). I now believe that it *was* a test, but not, as conventionally understood, a test of Abraham's willingness to obey without questioning. As I now read the story, God speaks twice to Abraham, once telling him to take the boy's life and a second time telling him to spare the child. The test is to see if Abraham will be able to distinguish the true voice of God from the inauthentic. It would seem that God chose Abraham to give humanity a fresh start precisely because He saw in Abraham an innate sense of righteousness, and this would test whether Abraham truly deserved that distinction. Will he be wise enough to know that the call to compassion is the authentic voice of God and the call to murder is a distortion?

As God tested Abraham thousands of years ago, I believe that God is testing us today, to see if we have learned to recognize God's true voice amid the clamor of so many voices claiming to speak for God. Will we have absorbed the spirit and message of the Sanctuary that is a haven and a respite from the clash of arms and the shedding of blood?

I believe that God is looking for Muslims who will say No to those who speak falsely in God's name: No, I have read the Koran, and I find there a God who cherishes life and protects the innocent.

I believe that God is looking for Christians who will say No to those preachers who claim that anyone who disagrees with them is the enemy. The Christianity to which they turn for the salvation of their soul is a religion that centers on whom they are required to love, not whom they are entitled to hate.

And I believe that God is looking for Jews who will say No; when a Jew is asked to do something in the name of the Torah that makes him less of a mensch than the Torah calls on him to be, he will not do it.

There is one more weapon we can deploy in our personal battle against the threat of terrorism, and that is faith. Not faith that God will protect the innocent and make sure that nothing bad happens to them. We learned long before September 11 that we don't live in that kind of world. The faith I am talking about is the conviction that God has made the world in such a way that wicked people inevitably overreach and bring about their own downfall. Wickedness can do a great deal of damage but ultimately contains the seeds of its own defeat.

For much of World War II, Hitler was winning the war. He had conquered all of Western Europe and was threatening England. There were respectable voices urging the United States to accept Nazi domination of Europe as a fait accompli rather than send American troops overseas to take on the Nazi Wehrmacht. But Hitler lost because it is in the nature of evil people to continue doing harm until they go too far and are stopped. Hitler lost because, convinced by early victories that his army was invincible and bolstered by his belief that the Slavs were an inferior race, he violated his nonaggression pact with Stalin and invaded Russia. In addition, he diverted forces to a relatively minor skirmish in the Balkans, delaying his invasion of Russia to the point where his army, like Napoleon's, was trapped in a Russian winter. His fanatical anti-Semitism drove scores of world-class physicists who were loyal Germans, Einstein among them, to leave Germany for the United States, so that the atomic bomb was invented there rather than in Germany. In an act of misplaced loyalty with Japan, he declared war on the United States the day after Pearl Harbor, instantly uniting all Americans against him. On paper, Hitler had the military power to win a war against a Western coalition that was unprepared, mired in an economic depression, and exhausted after the bloodletting of World War I barely twenty years earlier. He succeeded in causing immense harm and the deaths of millions, but ultimately he lost because he could not control his appetite for conquest and destruction. I believe that the forces behind the attack on New York City and Washington on 9/11, forces that lust for world domination in the name of a fanatical version of their religion, will follow a similar trajectory: Their early success against an unprepared victim will ultimately lead to defeat, because I believe that God's world is made in such a way that it will not tolerate evildoers for long.

How then shall we confront a world marred by the threat of terrorism? Much as we deal with the threat of other dangers, by seeing the danger posed by terrorism realistically but optimistically. We should be alert but not frightened, vigilant but not paranoid. We may have to accept the sad reality that here and there innocent people will die at the hands of terrorists despite our best efforts and the best efforts of governments and religious leaders, even as we have learned to live with the damage done by automobile accidents, tainted food and water, and shortages of medicine in some parts of the world. It is tragic, it is unfair, and it is certainly not the will of God. Such things cast a shadow over God's world but not a big enough shadow to prevent those untouched by it from embracing life to the fullest. We will have to hold on to our faith that God has given us a world in which evil is possible but evil will ultimately consume itself. We will play our music in the dark until the lights come back on. In the Ninety-second Psalm, the psalmist compares the wicked to grass, which grows quickly and then shrivels and dies, and compares the righteous to a slow-growing but long-living palm tree or a cedar of Lebanon. He writes,

> Though the wicked sprout like grass and evildoers flourish,
> They are destined to be destroyed forever.
>
> (PSALM 92:7)

3

God Was Not in the Hurricane

THE FEAR OF NATURAL DISASTER

> There was a mighty wind, splitting mountains and shat-
> tering rocks, but the Lord was not in the wind. After the
> wind, an earthquake, but the Lord was not in the earth-
> quake. After the earthquake, a fire, but the Lord was not
> in the fire. And after the fire, a still, small voice.
>
> I KINGS 19:11–12

In 1989, I found myself caught in a major earthquake in San Francisco, registering 6.9 on the Richter scale. I was stand-ing in front of a restaurant, ready to have an early dinner at five o'clock and watch the World Series on the restaurant's tele-vision, when I felt the sidewalk begin to buckle and shake beneath my feet. There are probably few experiences more unsettling than feeling the ground you are standing on give way. I didn't know what to do, whether it would be safer to remain outdoors and take my chances or run into a building where the ceiling could collapse and bury me. In the few sec-onds I had to make up my mind, I vaguely remembered having read something about standing in a doorway during an earth-quake, but I couldn't recall if that was what you were supposed to do or what you should avoid doing. I ran into the restaurant and hid under a table until it was over. The quake probably lasted less than a minute, though it felt longer to me. I felt at the mercy of a force well beyond my control, with nothing I could do to protect myself except to hope I would be one of the lucky ones.

Walking back to my hotel, I could see collapsed buildings in downtown San Francisco and fires breaking out in the hills around the city. Traffic lights were not working; automobile traffic was minimal. There was an eerie emptiness to the downtown area of one of America's most vibrant cities.

Predictably, in the days following, I heard religious leaders "explain" the earthquake as God's righteous judgment on San Francisco's distinctively liberal lifestyle. I could have told them that the fires and the fallen buildings I saw were mostly in neighborhoods that were not centers of the activities that so upset the morality police. For understandable reasons, natural disasters tend to hurt poor people more than affluent ones, causing more damage to vulnerable shacks and mobile home parks than to substantial mansions, hurting the underinsured more than the adequately insured, the economically marginal more than those who had the resources to flee to hotels in other cities. I will not accept, I will not even consider the answer given by some religious leaders that these natural events were sent as a divine punishment, an echo of the Flood in the time of Noah, when God grew so disgusted with human wickedness that He resolved to wash the world clean and start over. I have heard some preachers tell their congregations that these terrible things were a sign of God's wrath at a society that banished prayer from the public schools, afforded a measure of dignity to homosexuals, or considered partitioning the Holy Land between Israelis and Palestinians, and I thought to myself, How dare they claim to be able to read God's mind and see these horrible calamities as God's will! Couldn't these events as easily be seen as God's righteous judgment on clergymen who take His name in vain to endorse their political opinions?

When the earthquake was over and I realized that I had not been harmed, my first thought was, Thank God I'm all right. Then my second thought, a moment later, was, Wait a minute. What do I mean by that? Do I believe that God chose me to be saved while others perished and am I thanking Him for favoring me? I don't believe that. The earthquake struck exactly a week after Yom Kippur, when we recite the formula "It is decided on Rosh HaShanah and confirmed on Yom Kippur who shall live and who shall die, who by fire and who by drowning, who by famine and who by earthquake." For decades, I had taught my congregants not to take those words literally. I don't believe that it is determined in September whether I will live through the entire coming year. But here I was, a week after Yom Kippur, thanking God for designating me as one who would live, bringing me safely through an earthquake. After a moment's reflection, I realized that "Thank God I'm all right" was not really a theological statement crediting God with my safety. It was a spontaneous outburst of relief phrased in theological language by a religiously inclined person.

My sense is that there is nothing that reaches more deeply into our souls than the experience of facing danger and being spared. In biblical times, a person would bring an offering of gratitude when he had averted disaster, different from and more elaborate than the offering he would bring to celebrate something joyous. In today's synagogue, the custom is to offer a special prayer of thanks for having been delivered from danger. When I returned to my home and my congregation on the Sabbath following the earthquake, I arranged to be called to the Torah so that I might recite that special prayer, praising God "who treats us better than we deserve." I felt that I had experienced something deeply religious, not that God had singled me out while condemning others to harm and that I should thank Him for it but that I had received a precious gift I had not earned. Escaping harm in a natural disaster was something beyond my control. Neither righteous behavior nor any record of philanthropy on my part could have guaranteed my safety. To say "Thank God I'm all right" is different from actually thanking God for being all right. It is an outburst of relief and deliverance. My prayer at the Torah after my safe return, the implication that I had sensed God's presence in that narrow escape, was my way of acknowledging that sometimes, but not always, fortune favors the innocent, and when it does, it would be a sin to believe that it happened because I deserved it.

In recent years, it has often seemed that the earth has been turning on its inhabitants with unprecedented, savage fury, leaving many people wondering just how livable some parts of our planet are. An undersea earthquake in the Pacific introduced us to the word "tsunami," a giant tidal wave that killed a quarter of a million people in several countries, wiped out entire towns and villages, and left millions more homeless. Survivors asked interviewers where they were supposed to go when there was nothing left of their village. Massive earthquakes struck populated areas in Iran, China, and Pakistan, leaving tens of thousands dead and bringing misery to many more. I remember seeing on the faces of survivors that same look of bafflement that comes from learning that you cannot count on the earth under your feet to remain stable. In our own country, a series of blows from category 5 hurricanes, among the strongest on record, virtually washed away a major American city and inundated several smaller ones, leaving scores dead and hundreds of thousands homeless.

In Florida, synagogues had to cancel High Holy Day services because of impending hurricanes, the equivalent of churches canceling Christmas prayers in a blizzard. In 2005, for the first time in history, the agency that tracks hurricanes and tropical storms and gives each a name in alphabetical order ran out of names and had to use letters from the Greek alphabet as the hurricane season continued past its usual fall termination on November 30.

A friend of mine who lives in Florida and had to board up his house repeatedly because of storm warnings sent me a newspaper clipping that read: "How To Survive A Florida Hurricane: (1) Fill your car's tank with gas. (2) Buy four days' worth of food and water. (3) Drive to Indiana."

But I am not sure that even that advice will buy a person immunity from natural disaster. The Great Plains states suffered from tornadoes, the Southwest from drought that left it vulnerable to forest fires, and the West Coast experienced record rainfall, mudslides, and flooding. It would seem there is no place where one can be safe from the wrath of weather. Of late, people in all parts of the country have been wondering why God created a world in which such things could happen so often and cause so much misery.

It is one thing to accept the unpleasant truth that there are evil people in the world who are intent on doing harm to others. Evil people can be identified and isolated. But how do we come to terms with the possibility of Mother Nature's turning against us? We can minimize the risk of violent crime by staying close to home and avoiding dangerous neighborhoods. But what can we do about the threat of flood, fire, tornado, or earthquake reaching us where we live? What can we do when the water we depend on for life and the fire we depend on for warmth turn on us and become agents of destruction?

While some insisted on understanding the destruction of New Orleans in the wake of Hurricane Katrina as God's judgment on a city notorious for its scandalous behavior, there too, as in San Francisco, it was the poorest families, the poorest neighborhoods, that suffered disproportionately. Unless one believes that God loves rich people more than poor people (and only someone who has never read either the Hebrew Bible or the New Testament could believe that), it makes no sense to justify these calamities as God's wrath called down on sinners. A colleague of mine who visited New Orleans shortly after the calamity reported that many people attributed what happened to the city as God's judgment on a notoriously corrupt government and a venal police force. "But if that was the cause of this destruction and this suffering," he went on to write, "I don't understand why so many churches, large and small, were swept away in this flood."

What are we talking about when we ask whether natural disasters are the will of God? To the person who does not believe "His eye is on the sparrow," the person who does not believe that everything that happens in life is an expression of God's will, this entire discussion may seem little more than a word game. Have we nothing better to do when disaster strikes than sit around quibbling about theology? As I understand it, to ask, Was the hurricane or the tsunami the will of God? is not really a question about God. It is not asking, Was God pleased or saddened when the flood nearly destroyed New Orleans? It is a question about the kind of world we live in. Does our world make sense? Does everything happen for a reason? For many people, the only way to go on believing that our world is a safe and reliable one is to insist that the hurricane is in fact an "act of God," that there is a moral reason for every natural disaster and every malignant tumor even if we cannot understand it, that everything is part of some overall plan. It is a very comforting answer to many people. But it is one I cannot affirm. It requires us to say of Nature's victims, "They must have done something to deserve it," and to say when we are the victims, "I must have done something to deserve it." Or, if we want to be more charitable, "What happened to them (and me) was undeserved, but it must be intended to lead to a greater good that we in our limited wisdom cannot discern."

The problem is, seeing these shattering events as God's doing not only insults the victims by implying that they deserved what happened to them. It not only robs them of their right to feel outraged at the unfairness of what happened to them. It insults God as well. In his book *A Grief Observed*, C. S. Lewis wrote, shortly after his wife's death of cancer, that the danger of affirming all misfortune as God's will is not so much that people will stop believing in God. The danger is that they will continue to believe in God but will believe terrible things about Him. Worse than concluding "there is no God," people will conclude that there is a God and He is a monster. He is a cruel, heartless God who snatches children from their families and takes parents from children who need them, a God who uses His awesome power to destroy in an hour what took a family years to build. Who can love a God like that? Who can turn to such a God for help in times of grief? Such a God would be a God who inspires fear, not a God who repeatedly urges His people, "Don't be afraid."

Others, unwilling to believe in a cruel, capricious God, make sense of natural disasters by claiming that God is not responsible for them; people are. We have seen human beings in their greed and thoughtlessness build homes where it is not safe to build them, on geological fault lines, on cliff sides, at the water's edge in a hurricane zone. We have seen people live in homes vulnerable to storms or mudslides because there was no other housing available to them and then feel doubly victimized when those homes fall victim to natural events. We have bulldozed the rain forests and polluted the air with our factories and automobiles, changing the climate in the process, so that nearly all of the wettest and driest years on record have occurred in the past two decades, and then, when misfortune strikes, we ask, How could this happen to me?

Blaming ourselves rather than God has the virtue of leaving us free to turn to God for help and relieves us of the sense of helplessness that can paralyze us and make a frightening situation that much more frightening. If we helped make it happen, we can do something about it. We can prevent future occurrences. But how much can we in fact do? We can locate our homes more rationally, but more people are being born all the time and more people are living longer, and we all need somewhere to live. We can take steps to blunt the impact of global warming, which threatens to melt the ice caps and warm the oceans, making hurricanes more powerful and raising the sea level until coastal cities, home to millions of people, lie underwater. Many people are trying to do something, by driving hybrid cars and taking public transportation, by demanding laws to control industrial pollution. One Chicago cabdriver, while unloading a passenger's luggage from the trunk of his cab, realized how bad the exhaust fumes he was inhaling must be for his health and for the environment. He organized workshops for his fellow cabbies on ways to reduce idling and pollution, for their own good and that of their community. But it is hard to ask people to give up the comfort of air-conditioning and the convenience of one car per person in order to achieve a minuscule reduction in our environmental impact, unless we know that everyone else is also doing the same thing. Moreover, it ill behooves the industrialized nations of the world to tell other nations that we are entitled to large homes, cars, and factories but they are not.

When we look at what we are doing to the planet we live on, we realize that there are a lot of big and little things that we can do that will help, and there is one thing we can do that will make things worse. That is to be so overwhelmed by fear and helplessness that we do nothing.

In all likelihood, we are destined to live in a world where hurricanes, earthquakes, floods, fires, and famines will continue to occur, and television news will continue to bring images of suffering and destruction into our living rooms. Unwilling to blame God and uncomfortable accepting guilt and responsibility ourselves, how shall we make sense of these terrible events?

I can give you the answer in six words: God is moral; Nature is not. Nature is blind, uncaring, incapable of distinguishing between good people and bad ones, between the deserving and the undeserving. I believe that when God created the natural world, He blessed it with beauty and precision. He gave us an orderly world, one in which we can predict to the minute when the sun will rise and set in a given city on a given date years from now. He gave us a world capable of stirring our souls with its beauty, the serenity of a rainbow, the majesty of a mountain, the magic of quietly falling snow. Even the destructive aspects of Nature, including the earthquakes and the hurricanes, are not random events. They follow natural laws that we may one day understand sufficiently to be better able to anticipate them and limit their damage.

But when God created the natural world, He withheld from it one blessing that He shared only with you and me: the ability to know the difference between good and bad, between morally right and morally wrong. Human beings are able (or should be able) to do that, but we can't expect animals or forces of nature to be able to. To me, that is the meaning of the story of Adam and Eve tasting the fruit of the Tree of the Knowledge of Good and Evil.

A falling rock is simply obeying the law of gravity. There is no way it can know whether the person in its path deserves to be hit by a rock or not. A speeding bullet will cause serious injury to anyone it strikes, whether that person is an enemy soldier, an escaping murderer, a martyred president, or an innocent bystander. It is blind, amoral physics, not God's choice. Responsibility lies with the person who threw the stone or fired the bullet, not with the stone or bullet itself and not with God who established the unchanging laws of Nature that do not make exceptions for nice people.

A personal story: The synagogue in St. Thomas in the U.S. Virgin Islands is the second-oldest synagogue in the Western Hemisphere, having been established in 1796. Only the one in Curaçao is older. In the early years of the twentieth century, my father's two sisters and their husbands left their native

Lithuania and moved to St. Thomas. There they settled, prospered, and became mainstays of the synagogue. As the congregation approached the bicentennial anniversary of their synagogue's founding, they invited me to be the featured speaker at the celebration. My wife and I were looking forward to a tropical vacation. Then, in the late fall of 1995, St. Thomas was struck by a powerful hurricane. When we arrived in January 1996, we surveyed the damage. There was hardly a functioning hotel to house us. More than half of the homes on the island were in need of major repair (this on an island where every board and nail has to be shipped in from overseas). Electricity was available only sporadically, and telephone service was unreliable. The young rabbi of the synagogue told us that on the night of the hurricane a neighbor who lived on the first floor of their building urged him to bring his family down from their third-floor apartment and stay with them. Fortunately, they heeded his advice, because the upper floors collapsed during the storm and only the first floor was left intact. The two-hundred-year-old synagogue escaped damage, though the building next door, used as a social hall, was reduced to rubble.

It was clear to me that when I spoke at the synagogue's bicentennial on a Friday night, I would have to abandon the speech I had prepared and address the devastation wrought by the hurricane. After paying tribute to the founders of the synagogue and acknowledging the presence of my relatives, I told the congregation a story from the biblical book of Kings, a story about the prophet Elijah.

Elijah lived in the ninth century B.C.E., a time of material prosperity but moral decay. A king named Ahab cemented an alliance with the king of Tyre (in today's Lebanon) by marrying the Tyrian king's daughter Jezebel. The alliance led to unprecedented prosperity for some people and to the importation of the queen's religion, the worship of the fertility cult of Baal. Israelite society was characterized by religious laxity, idol worship, and economic disparity, precisely the qualities that prompted the appearance of those great champions of morality whom we know as the prophets.

It was at this time that Elijah appeared as a spokesman for the God of Moses and of Mt. Sinai, where the Ten Commandments had been given. King Ahab turned on Elijah, killing most of those who dared to follow him and threatening Elijah's life as well. In despair, fearing not so much for his own life as for the future of his faithless people, Elijah fled to the Sinai wilderness, returning to the mountain where God had originally sealed His covenant with Israel, to seek the presence and guidance of God.

There, in chapter 19 of the first book of Kings, we read: "There was a mighty wind, splitting mountains and shattering rocks, but the Lord was not in the wind. After the wind, an earthquake, but the Lord was not in the earthquake. After the earthquake, a fire, but the Lord was not in the fire. And after the fire, a still, small voice" (1 Kings 19:11–12). The voice commanded Elijah to go back to Israel. There were things he could do, people he could rally to his side to redeem his country.

For me, the key words in the story are "the Lord was not in the wind." God did not send the hurricane, I told the people of St. Thomas. God did not destroy your homes or knock down your trees. The hurricane was not an act of God. It was an act of Nature, blind, unfeeling Nature, which can be so beautiful one day and so destructively cruel the next.

But if God was not in the hurricane, where was He to be found? You will find God, I told them, in your response to the hurricane. You will find God in the still, small voice that is almost drowned out in the noise of blame and recrimination, the voice that urges you to pick up the broken pieces of your homes, of your community, of your lives and see if you can put them back together again.

A year after Hurricane Katrina virtually washed away New Orleans, I was invited to visit the city to view the damage and the reconstruction efforts and offer some words of encouragement to its residents, addressing a gathering that filled a local house of worship that had not been damaged. I told the people the story of Elijah on Mt. Sinai, how the prophet found God not in the storm or in the earthquake or in the fire, but in the still, small voice that told him to go back home because there were things for him to do there. To his anguished cry of "Why?" God responded not with an explanation but with an agenda. That is what you do after a tragedy. You don't explain it. You don't justify it. You survive it and go on living, and you look for ways to put your life together again.

God was not in the storm, I told them. That was Nature. God was not in the selfish, self-justifying behavior of so many people who responded badly to the crisis. That was human nature at its least human. But God's was the still, small voice that prompted so many people to respond bravely, generously, unselfishly—from people who risked their own lives to save others to people who opened their hearts, their homes, and their purses in an effort to help. It was God who prompted hundreds of college students to spend their spring break rebuilding homes for strangers in Louisiana and Mississippi instead of partying on a beach somewhere, and inspired members of the Rotary Club of Pass Christian, Mississippi, to devote their weekly luncheon meeting to repairing homes in their stricken community. Nature has no choice; it can only follow its own built-in laws. But human beings, confronting a natural disaster, can choose how they will respond. This is the enduring lesson psychiatrist Victor Frankl learned from his years in Auschwitz: You cannot control what happens to you, but you can always control how you respond to what happens to you.

Finally, I urged my New Orleans audience to focus on what they still had left and not only on what they had lost. I told them the story of the family whose house was destroyed in a fire. They were huddled together on the sidewalk when a well-meaning woman came by and said to them, "Oh, you poor people. You don't have a home anymore." The young boy in the family replied, "Oh no, we still have a home. We just don't have a house to put it in." Victims of floods, fires, earthquakes, and hurricanes may lose their possessions, but if they survive, they still have their homes even if they lack a house to put those homes in.

And we, who are only spectators at other people's misfortune, how shall we respond? We can send money, food, blankets. We can send our prayers. But there is something more that we need to do. We need to go beyond seeing the people struck by natural disasters, whether in Indonesia, Bangladesh, or New Orleans, solely as victims, as objects of our pity and recipients of our charity. We need to see them as being much like ourselves, human beings vulnerable to the caprice of Nature. When our only response is pity, when we see these people only as victims, the danger is that we will distance ourselves from them psychologically, dividing the world into "they" who suffer and "we" who magnanimously reach out to help. The truth is that when it comes to vulnerability to the destructive forces of Nature and other misfortunes, there is no "them" and "us." There is only "us," the vast human family linked by our shared vulnerability that makes no distinction as to race, religion, or economic level. Some who satisfy themselves behind acts of generosity, comforting themselves with the thought that "all will be well with me because I am a good person," are forgetting that so much misfortune is a matter of good or bad luck, not good or bad behavior.

Martin Buber, in commenting on the biblical verse "You shall love your neighbor as yourself" (Leviticus 19:18), offers this image: Imagine yourself peeling an apple. You are holding the apple in your left hand and the knife in your right. Suddenly the knife slips and wounds the hand holding the apple. Should the right hand feel relieved that it is the left hand that is bleeding? Should it be pleased that it was spared? Should it look at the left hand as an alien limb to be pitied? Of course not; both hands are part of the same body. When one hand is hurt, the entire body feels the pain. That, says Buber, is the meaning of the biblical commandment. Our neighbor is part of us. When any human being suffers, it should be a source of pain to all of us. We should feel pain, not pity.

People who have been hit by calamities, who may have lost family members, homes, irreplaceable possessions, are not simply victims. In many cases, they are heroes, people who have shown resourcefulness, resilience, courage, and the determination to rebuild what Nature destroyed.

This then is what the still, small voice of God says to all of us who share life on this awesome but unpredictable planet: To those who have been hurt by natural disaster, God says, Don't be afraid. The earthquake was not God's doing. The hurricane was not God's doing. That was blind, uncaring Nature. But God is neither blind nor uncaring. Maybe He can't protect you from the devastation, but He can keep you from being devastated by it. Wind and rain can tear apart a house, but they need not destroy a home because a home is not a building. A home is not furniture. A home is people bound to each other by bonds of love. Earthquakes can reduce churches and shrines to rubble, but they cannot shatter faith, for the roots of faith lie too deep for the earthquake to reach. You will ask, Why? but God says, I will not explain or try to justify. Instead of an answer, I will give you an agenda of things to do. I will give you all the strength, all the courage, all the faith you need to rebuild and go on with your lives. And that will be the miracle.

And to those of us who watch the devastation from afar, there is a still, small voice that says to us, Don't be afraid to share other people's pain and vulnerability. We can handle it. Don't let geographical distance translate into emotional distance. It wasn't God's decision that the disaster should strike their community and not yours. God's promise is, Should you one day find yourself in a situation in which you will need special strength to go on, I will give you that strength. If you cannot rebuild your life by yourself, I will inspire people to come to your aid even as I am inspiring people to reach out to the victims you read about. Yes, it is a scary world out there, but you will not have to find your way through it alone, for I will be with you.

4

*

Suddenly Nothing Is the Same

THE FEAR OF RAPID CHANGE

> Future shock: the shattering stress and disorientation
> that we induce in individuals by subjecting them to too
> much change in too short a time.
>
> ALVIN TOFFLER, *Future Shock*

In the 1980s, ivory was fetching such a high price that criminal elements in Botswana, home to some of Africa's greatest elephant herds, saw the chance to get rich by killing elephants for their tusks. They targeted primarily full-grown adult elephants, whose tusks were the largest. By the time the authorities cracked down on the poaching and world governments banned trade in ivory, an astonishing 90 percent of the adult elephants in many herds had been killed, leaving communities of immature elephants without adult leadership to teach them how to behave.

In their book *Secrets of the Savanna,* Mark and Delia Owens describe the results: "As with humans, adult elephants keep some sense of order and peace within their strongly bonded families. . . . However, in North Luangwa, a third of the family groups had no [adults] older than fifteen years because they had been shot. [Many] groups were made up

57

entirely of unsupervised, inexperienced and unruly teenagers, some all females, some all males, roaming around on their own in an elephant version of *Lord of the Flies.* . . . As a result of this change, the family units of North Luangwa were less cohesive and the adolescents more aggressive than in populations that had not suffered from poaching."

What the Owenses learned by watching the elephants, and what I learned by reading their book, is that the social structure of a society, whether animal or human, breaks down when there are no adults available to model mature, decent behavior for the youngsters in their midst. The story of human society from the time our ancestors lived in caves has involved the older generations teaching the younger generations what the elders had learned from their elders, with the younger generation depending on them to teach them what they needed to know. Remove that role modeling and chaos ensues. (The Owenses reported that the mere presence of an adult bull elephant lowers testosterone levels in young males by 10 percent.)

As I read the Owenses' account of elephant behavior, I thought not only of human populations ravaged by war, where the adults had been killed or taken off to the army and children were left to fend for themselves. I thought of communities where poverty, unemployment, and drug addiction had left young people growing up with absent or ineffective parents. But I thought too of the waves of immigrants who arrived in the United States from Central and Southern Europe in the mid-nineteenth century and from Eastern Europe as the nineteenth century blended into the twentieth. Much of the time, parents were present but ineffectual. They typically could not speak the language and could not get a decent job or had to work far from home. As a result, many families experienced a loss of parental authority. Adolescents who had better command of the language and knew their way around often found little reason to listen to their elders. Many of these ethnic youths formed gangs that disregarded law and custom, even as the teenage male elephants of Botswana did, and their bewildered parents felt helpless to do anything about it. They were strangers in an alien world.

Then it occurred to me that this pattern of social disruption was not limited to geographical immigrants. When circumstances change so rapidly that adults experience a sense of "future shock," when the implements and vocabulary of society change radically in a short time, many parents feel like strangers in their own land. Parents have less to teach and are less confident about trying to teach it, and children feel they have less reason to listen.

I know that feeling all too well. When I am having problems with my computer or when I want to use my cell phone for something more complicated than making a call, I have to turn to my teenage grandson for help. (I've been doing it since he was eight.) In the world of modern electronic devices, I am an immigrant. I don't speak the language. I have no idea how they work or what is going wrong when they don't work. Having grown up with computers and video games, my grandson can usually set things right in a matter of seconds. I am proud of his facility with computers (don't we all overvalue things that we find difficult?), and I appreciate his willingness to come to my rescue, but I can't help feeling that there is something out of joint about the pattern, that *I* should be the one helping *him* learn to do things. I am mindful of the rabbinic teaching "Learning from the young is like eating unripe fruit and drinking newly pressed wine, while learning from the old is like eating ripe fruit and drinking aged wine." Yet in this technologically complicated world, we seem to have no choice but to learn from the young. Future shock has created a mirror image of a stable society, a world in which knowledge flows from the young to the old. And I can't help feeling that, as with the elephants of Botswana, something valuable has been lost in the process.

Change is unsettling; we crave the familiar. Every priest or minister, every rabbi or cantor knows that. We can preach the most radical sermon and people will listen politely. But let the cantor or organist change a favorite melody, let the custodian rearrange the seats, and we will hear the discontent. We like to return to our favorite vacation spots, and we are upset if we don't find them exactly as we remember them. Professor Robert Sapolsky of Stanford has found from his research that if you have not learned to like certain foods by your early thirties, chances are you will never like them, and the music you will enjoy most throughout your life will be the music you listened to in your twenties. In his book *Monkeyluv,* Sapolsky writes, "[Even] the great creative minds . . . are less open to someone else's novelty. Think of Einstein fighting a rearguard action against quantum mechanics."

Recent discoveries in neuroscience help us to understand these reactions. According to science, all living creatures crave what is known as homeostasis, when things remain the same. Our brains register serious discomfort when things aren't what and where we expect them to be. It is a lot more efficient to be able to do things the way you have always done them, without having to think about it. (Think of suddenly encountering a detour on your familiar drive home.) As a result, we tend to resist change even when change would seem to be for our benefit.

But for many people, change can be more than just unpleasant or unsettling. It can be terrifying. It can carry the threat of serious loss, the danger that something we have cherished will be taken from us. I remember what it felt like as a twelve-year-old boy leaving my neighborhood school and heading off to middle school, a larger world farther from home and filled with strangers. At a time when my body was starting to change, the world I lived in daily was changing as well. Will people like me? Will I make friends? Will the work be too hard? Now imagine a slightly older child moving to a new city because her father has changed jobs. The school is new. The neighborhoods are new. New ways of doing things need to be learned. She has nothing familiar to fall back on. She is entering a world in which most others her age already have their friends. How will she fit in?

Think of an older couple, perhaps finding themselves "empty nesters," perhaps anticipating retirement. They are preparing to sell their home, leaving behind all the memories attached to it, and to move to smaller quarters. They worry that their world is shrinking around them not only physically but emotionally and psychologically. With every major purchase they make, they wonder if this will be the last car, the last television set they will ever own. And if they should survive to a ripe age, they worry about outliving their savings.

Change always means giving up the familiar for the unknown. To the average working man or woman in an industry in flux, change is more likely to mean unemployment than promotion. To a middle-aged man or woman, a change in one's medical condition is more likely to be a cause for concern than for satisfaction. Like an earthquake, rapid change renders the ground under our feet unstable. Things are out of our control, changing too fast for us to keep up with them. Change threatens to render us irrelevant, no longer competent, no longer in a position to speak with authority and pass our wisdom on to others. That wisdom is being devalued even as we watch.

In 1993, the scientist Alan Lightman wrote a little book of fictional sketches entitled *Einstein's Dreams*. The premise of the book is that while Albert Einstein was formulating his theory of relativity, he was so obsessed with the idea that people could experience the passage of time differently that at night he dreamed of alternative universes where time operated differently than it does in our world. He dreamed of a world, for example, where time flowed backward, where people were born old and grew younger day by day until they died by disappearing into their mothers' wombs. He imagined a world where time passed more slowly at higher elevations, so that rich people built tall buildings on mountaintops and lived on the top floor in the hope of thereby living a few days longer. The chapter that impressed me most was centered on Lightman's concept of "the still point in time."

He writes, "There is a place where time stands still. Raindrops hang motionless in air. Pendulums of clocks float midswing. Dogs raise their muzzles in silent howls. Pedestrians are frozen on the dusty streets, their legs cocked as if held by strings. . . . For this is the center of time. From this place, time travels outward in concentric circles—at rest at the center, slowly picking up speed at greater diameters.

"Who would make pilgrimage to the center of time? Parents with children, and lovers."

Why "parents with children, and lovers"? Because they are prime examples of people for whom the current moment is so perfect that they want to hold on to it and never let it change. (The hero of Goethe's *Faust* is willing to sell his soul to the devil for the power to stop time, to be able to say, "This moment is so lovely, let it remain.") Lovers are afraid of change, afraid that change will mean the loss of love. When everything seems perfect, there is no way to go but down. Parents of young children will often fear the transformation of their sweet, cuddly eight-year-old into a surly, uncommunicative adolescent who is embarrassed to be seen with them and is vulnerable to all the dangers of adolescence.

Change makes us uncomfortable; change means loss of control, but change is inevitable. The Greek philosopher Heraclitus proclaimed two thousand years ago that "nothing endures but change." The Buddha taught his disciples to prepare for change by saying to themselves, "Everything I hold dear will one day change and be taken from me." If change is going to come anyway, wouldn't it make more sense, and make our lives easier, for us to get over our fears and learn to accept the inevitable, even to welcome it? After all, would we really want our children to remain eight years old and never grow up? Parents of a difficult, rebellious teenager may lament what they are living through, until they meet a family with a child who will never grow up and pass through adolescence, either fated to die young or afflicted with a severe developmental disability.

I may be nostalgic for the world I grew up in, Brooklyn in the 1940s, a world of stable neighborhoods, stable jobs, and stable marriages, until I remember that that superficial stability rested on the assumption that blacks, Jews, and women would "know their place" and not aspire to too much, that people born gay would live a life of pretense and denial, and that people trapped in abusive or unsatisfying marriages would endure them rather than face social disapproval. There is a lot about that world that I miss, but there is much about the things that have changed since then that I welcome and even celebrate. It was a world in which clergy and members of the several most prominent religions would rarely speak to members of different faiths. I am certain that the rabbi of my youth, a wonderful, open-minded man, did not know a single Christian clergyman on a first-name basis. A generation later, I can think of dozens of Christian clergy I consider good friends. I remember my father coming home from the office one day and telling us that a colleague of his had died and the man's Roman Catholic employees had been told by their priests not to attend his funeral in a synagogue because that would mean participating in a non-Catholic worship service. Today rabbis routinely officiate at bar mitzvah services, weddings, and funerals where the congregations predictably include a substantial number of non-Jews.

Our children are growing up in a very different world from the one their parents grew up in, which makes it harder for them to look to their parents for guidance. Half of all marriages today are ended by divorce. Gays and lesbians are "out," and their commitment ceremonies are reported on the society pages of the newspapers. The election of an African American to Congress or as CEO of a major corporation attracts far less attention today than did the Brooklyn Dodgers' signing of Jackie Robinson in 1947. Even the election of an African American president in 2008 was seen more as the culmination of a process than as a revolutionary change. I think of the scene in *West Side Story* in which Doc, the well-meaning pharmacist, tries to calm the rage of one of the teenage gangs in the neighborhood by saying to its members, "When I was your age . . . ," only to have the gang leader tell him, "You were never our age." He means, of course, that the challenges he and his friends face growing up are so different from what Doc faced at that age that Doc's experience has nothing to say to him. He is partly right but also significantly wrong. Some truths about life don't change even if technology and social mores change around us (which is why Leonard Bernstein could adapt Shakespeare's sixteenth-century play *Romeo and Juliet* to fit twentieth-century New York). Issues like respect for the life and feelings of others and the importance of maintaining one's integrity in the face of temptation are not that different just because we live in a world of computers and jet travel. I would like to be able to teach those truths to today's computer-literate young people, but I am afraid that they, like many of us before them, will scorn the lessons of the past and insist on learning those lessons for themselves.

Change can be good or bad and is often both at the same time. I am grateful for the medical advances of recent years, for computers and e-mail and jet travel. I celebrate the end of racial segregation and the passage of laws against sexual harassment instead of shrugging it off with the cliché "boys will be boys." But at the same time, I lament an economy that uses people up and discards them, a culture in which movie and television producers compete in a "race to the bottom" to see whose mindless vulgarity will draw larger audiences, and an ecology that puts meat on our tables by treating cows and chickens as if they were not living, sentient creatures and offers us food from factories instead of from fields and farms.

And sometimes, like so many things in life, a change can be

simultaneously good and bad. I remember reading an article about one of the inventors of the transistor. He had been driving to a conference where he was to be honored for his work when he pulled in to a rest stop and saw a family of four having lunch, each one listening to his or her individual music player, none of them talking to one another. He realized that his invention, which had done so much good, had also changed some things for the worse.

In the final analysis, however, the question of whether change is good or bad has to take second place to the undeniable fact that change simply is. Change happens and will continue to happen, and the real question is: Will we fear it or will we welcome it?

One of the ways in which people cope with future shock, the sense of unease induced by a world that is changing too rapidly for them, is by turning to religion. It should not surprise us that, in times of change and social upheaval, some people turn especially to traditional religion as a source of comfort. When I was a rabbinical student in the 1950s, we anticipated that by the year 2000 there would be no Orthodox Jews left in America, because the population would be entirely native born and college educated, and everyone knew that native-born, college-educated Americans would reject orthodoxy. The prospect gave us no satisfaction. We felt it would diminish the strength of Judaism, but we saw it as inevitable. Across the street from my school, at Union Theological Seminary, where liberal Protestant ministers were educated, they anticipated with equal certitude that by the year 2000 there would be no more fundamentalist Christians in America, for similar reasons. But here we are in the twenty-first century, and the Orthodox synagogues and fundamentalist churches are flourishing. How can we understand this? How can we explain the phenomenon of college-educated Americans believing that the theory of evolution is groundless and our planet is less than six thousand years old because they hold the Bible to be the literal and inerrant word of God?

The rise of fundamentalism concerns me not because I consider Orthodox Judaism as "the competition" but because I see the rise of nonrational, even antirational faith as a flight from unwelcome reality, a reluctance to recognize the truths of science, psychology, and archaeology lest they conflict with the way we grew up thinking about the world. But reality doesn't go away if we don't like it. I believe that there has to be an emotional, nonrational dimension to life. I have long argued that dropping everything we don't understand from religion is like lifting the hood of your car and throwing away everything whose function you don't understand. You're left with a much neater, simpler scene, but your car won't go anywhere. When I speak to medical groups and hospice workers, I always stress the need for an emotional, nonrational dimension to the work they do. But at the same time I worry about ill people who rely on prayer and miracles rather than listening to their doctors. My religious faith is rooted in the Bible as the product of divine revelation, but my religious faith remains open to new truths, and if science indisputably tells me that the world is millions of years old and physics tells me that it was impossible for the sun to stand still (more properly, for the earth to stop revolving around the sun) in the time of Joshua, I must accept those truths.

I suspect that people are reaching out to traditional, unchanging religion as a corrective to a world in which things are changing too fast for them. Religions rooted in tradition are by definition conservative and slow to change. Much of their power comes from that familiarity, the reassuring knowledge that we are doing things as they have been done for generations before us, that weddings, first communions, bar mitzvahs, even funerals have us doing things as our parents and grandparents did and as we saw done when we were young. They represent an anchor of stability and a source of comfort in a world in which nothing else seems to be holding still. I have dealt with countless families in their time of bereavement, people who had no taste for religious ritual in their lives before that moment, who told me afterward how grateful they were to have the guidance of religion telling them what to do at a time like that, knowing that this is what their forebears had done with their grief. I have counseled couples who initially rejected the need for any religious ceremony at the time of their marriage or to welcome the birth of a child because they didn't believe in it. After they were talked into it by family, they told me how meaningful it had been for them.

There are few things harder than inventing a new religious ceremony. Ceremonies work because they are familiar. There are reasons why the prayers of the traditional liturgy have survived for centuries and why people turn to them for a degree of comfort. There are reasons why no one has found it necessary to rewrite the psalms and why linguistically more accurate versions of the Twenty-third Psalm, "The Lord is my shepherd," leave people wondering why someone thought they had to improve on it.

But the conservative tendency in traditional religion can be problematic when it causes people to refuse to acknowledge advances in scientific understanding (by challenging estimates of the age of the earth or by resisting the promise of stem cell research) or to object to progress as a violation of God's will, seeing anything new as automatically suspect. It can be problematic when its followers object to such innovations as women clergy or updated liturgical language not because of any deeply held principle but because it's not the way we've always done it. (Old Jewish joke: How many synagogue leaders does it take to change a lightbulb? Answer: You want to change that lightbulb? My grandfather donated that lightbulb!) It is at times like this, times like our own, that religious leaders and followers have to heed God's reassuring words "Don't be afraid" when facing a future that may be different from a hallowed and cherished past. After all, every religion was born in an act of innovation, a conscious and radical break with the past. Abraham rejected the idol worship of his family and society. Jesus challenged the forms and theological underpinnings of first-century Judaism. Buddha went far beyond the Hinduism of his day, and Mohammed called on Arabs to serve God differently than they had been taught to serve Him. Every society, like every living human body, shows itself to be healthy by constantly shedding dead cells and growing new ones.

Life would be simpler if we could counter the fear of change just by telling people, "Change is inevitable; get used to it." But if it were that easy, God would not have needed to admonish so many generations not to be afraid. For the most part, the people to whom God addressed those words were not weak, timorous souls. They were men and women of considerable courage. Abraham boldly left home and homeland to found a radically new way of understanding and serving God, but God had to remind him to "fear not." Prophets like Isaiah and Jeremiah had the courage to speak truth to power but needed similar reassurance from God. What was God saying to them, and to us, with those words in the Bible? Was He just saying that change happens and we should accept it, or was He saying something more than that?

There is a conversation I have had dozens of times over the years with members of my congregation: women whose husbands had left them for a younger woman, newly bereaved husbands in their sixties who realized they didn't know how to cook dinner or do laundry, eighteen-year-olds heading off to college and not sure if they could handle the challenges of college classrooms and dorms. I would say to them, "I'm not going to minimize the challenge you're facing. Your life is going to be very different. You are going to have to get used to doing things you are not accustomed to doing. But I am confident you will be able to handle this for two reasons: First, you've faced other, similar challenges and you have struggled, but you were able to handle them. Think of times when you had to do something you had never done before. Remember how intimidating it seemed, how you wondered if you would ever be able to get the hang of it, how often you were tempted to give it up. But you kept at it, and before long, you were doing it comfortably. And second, I've known other people who had to cope with what you are facing, people with less going for them than you have in terms of personal skills and family support, and they found their way through. I'm confident you'll be fine as well."

And in most cases, that is just what happened. The bereaved husband learned to cook and clean. The rejected wife regained her self-confidence and found friendship in the company of other single women and an occasional male friend. The college freshman came home for Thanksgiving having carved out for himself a comfortable role on campus. And each of them told me the same thing: You were right; it was hard but not as hard as I was afraid it would be.

For some people, the scariest thing about rapid change goes beyond new technology and changing mores. They are afraid of science and technology running rampant, afraid that our technical ability to do things will outpace our moral insights into whether those things should be done. Religion and ethics will always be a step or two behind the latest technological invention. People worry about biologists learning to clone human beings, either as "spare parts" for existing people or as a way of bypassing traditional modes of reproduction in an effort to create a superior race of humans. Because they have seen so many fanciful movie plots come true a few years later, they worry about developments anticipated in science-fiction books and movies, the creation of life-forms that will be part human and part animal, or part human and part machine. People have nightmares about the government coming up with drugs to control our minds or read our thoughts. And they ask, Where are the religious voices to protest and tell us that such things are not permissible?

The religious response to cutting-edge advances in biology, neuroscience, and other disciplines will have to rest on two principles. First, it is an abdication of responsibility for religious leaders to insist that if something has never been done before, it should not be done now. I don't believe it was ever the will of God that people suffer from polio and that we were thwarting God's will by finding a cure. I don't believe that God wants some women who yearn to be mothers to be denied the experience of bearing and raising children. I believe that healing the sick and relieving suffering are very much the will of God.

But at the same time, it is the obligation of religious leaders to insist that some religious teachings reflect eternal truths, that among them are the insistence on the dignity and uniqueness of every human being as the only creature fashioned in the image of God and the conviction that the ultimate sin is using another human being without regard for his or her well-being.

I believe that it is the moral obligation of scientists not to see religious spokesmen as improperly meddling in matters beyond their understanding. Scientists and theologians need to speak to each other as well as listen to each other with a measure of humility and mutual respect.

It is intimidating to have to change the way you do things because your world is changing around you. But it is far worse to live in a rapidly changing world and to be afraid to change with it. Are you afraid of change? Be more afraid of being unable to change. That is the scary part. Advertising executive and author Bruce Barton warned people, "When you are through changing, you're through." The Bible tells a story that should remind us of the dangers of being unable to change with changing circumstances. When God determines to destroy the irredeemably wicked cities of Sodom and Gomorrah (whose unforgivable sin, by the way, was not homosexuality but cruelty to strangers; see Ezekiel 16:49), He advises Abraham's nephew Lot and his family, the only decent people in the city, to flee Sodom and not look back (Genesis 19:17). But unlike Abraham, who marched willingly into an unknown future, Lot is hesitant to leave his familiar surroundings. He knows how depraved a community Sodom is, but it has been his home. He is used to it and does not know what life will be like outside it. He may feel he is too old to learn new ways and start over somewhere else. He virtually has to be dragged out of his house. Though God has warned the family to flee and not look back, Lot's wife cannot tear herself away and turns around for one last look, at which point, the Bible tells us, she is turned into a pillar of salt. Tourist guides at the Dead Sea today will point out the column of salt that was once, thousands of years ago, Mrs. Lot.

Why salt? There were so many other punishments that might have befallen her. I like to think that she turned to salt because salt is a preservative. In the premodern world, salt was used not so much to flavor food as to preserve it, to keep it from changing and spoiling. To live preserved in salt is the fate of people who are so bound to the past or so unsure of their ability to cope with the future that they continue to do what they have always done, even when it no longer fits the new circumstances in which they live.

Change is a law of life, and things seem to be changing faster in today's world than they did in the generations before ours. We can't hold back the tide of change any more than we can keep the sun from setting or the seasons from changing. All we can control is how well we respond to the changes, and on that question the Bible offers us two models. One is Lot and his wife, so afraid of an unknown future that they prefer to remain captives of a corrupt and limiting present. The other is Lot's uncle Abraham and Lot's cousin Jacob, each summoned to leave a relatively comfortable situation and step into a world being born, armed only with the confidence born of God's promise, "Do not fear, for I will be with you and your life will be a blessed one."

5

A World Without People

THE FEAR THAT HUMANITY WILL DESTROY ITSELF

> The earth was barren and nothing grew for there was no
> human being to work the field.
>
> GENESIS 2:5

By the fall of 1983, my book *When Bad Things Happen to Good People* had attracted the attention of several foreign publishers and was in the process of being translated into a dozen or more languages. (As I like to tell people, I have a shelf of books in my study that I wrote but cannot read.) The publishers of the German and Danish editions invited me to come to Europe to help promote the book in Munich and Copenhagen. The experience of speaking as a rabbi to a German audience about bad things happening to innocent victims less than forty years after the Holocaust was an unforgettable one. But it was in Copenhagen that I was asked a question that no one had ever asked me before.

I was speaking in the Great Synagogue of Copenhagen under the auspices of the chief rabbi of Denmark and the Danish Ministry of Culture. At the end of my lecture, which articulated my belief that God does not send, and cannot prevent, the tragedies that darken our lives but rather sends us the strength and grace we need to cope with them, a young woman asked me, "If people set out to destroy our planet in a nuclear war, do you believe that God would let that happen, or would He intervene to prevent it?" Her question was prompted by the United States having recently equipped its troops in West Germany with Pershing missiles capable of being armed with nuclear warheads. To us in the United States, it was just another incident in the Cold War. But to the Danes, whose country borders Germany, which was then still divided between East and West, it raised the prospect of a nuclear war erupting in their backyard.

I didn't know how to answer her. My experience as a religious leader had been exclusively with personal tragedies, not cosmic ones. I thought for a moment and, recalling my visit to the concentration camp in Dachau on the outskirts of Munich the previous day, I said to her and to the audience, "As I see it, history teaches us that if human beings are determined to do something cruel and destructive, we cannot depend on God to keep us from doing it. Only other human beings can prevent it. That should be the lesson of the Second World War. That is what human free will is all about. If we choose to do good, we get the credit. As the Talmud says, when a person does a good deed when he doesn't have to, God looks down and says, 'For this moment alone, it was worth creating the world.' But if we choose to do evil, to hurt one person or to hurt many people, we can't count on God to reach down and slap our hand away before it gets into the cookie jar. It seems to me that the history of my people and the history of your people should teach us that lesson."

At that point, the chief rabbi interrupted me to say that, with all deference to his distinguished American guest, he disagreed with me. He cited a verse from the book of Isaiah (45:18), "God who formed the earth and made it . . . He did not make it to be a wasteland but formed it for a habitation." That biblical promise reassured him that God would not permit the destruction of all life on earth. He referred to God's promise to Noah after the Flood: "Never again will I doom the earth because of Man" (Genesis 8:21). I was not about to enter into a theological disputation with the chief rabbi, who was a more distinguished religious leader and several decades my senior, in his synagogue, so I said only, "Amen, I pray that you are right," and went on to the next question.

But I have never forgotten that young woman's concern that human wrath and folly might put an end to human life on earth before she and her contemporaries would ever have the chance to experience it fully, to marry, to raise children, to embark on their careers, and I have never really shared the chief rabbi's confidence that God would not let it happen. I can understand why she was fearful. Her generation has been described in a letter to *The New Yorker* as "the first to take for granted the possibility, even the likelihood, of human extinction at our own hands." In 1983, when I spoke in Denmark, only a few governments had access to nuclear weapons, and they could be deterred by the knowledge that using them would inevitably lead to the destruction of their own country in retaliation. Today, such weapons can be found in the arsenals of several more governments, and many experts feel that the real danger of nuclear devastation comes from fanatical groups that might be able either to take over a government and its nuclear arsenal or to obtain those weapons on the black market. Such groups might not be deterred by the prospect of mutual suicide; indeed, they might welcome it.

I remember an incident when our daughter was about nine or ten years old. Shortly after midnight, there was a serious automobile accident on the highway close to our home. There was the loud noise of two cars colliding, followed by the sound of sirens from emergency vehicles. Our daughter ran into our bedroom, terrified that an atomic bomb had been dropped on our neighborhood and a nuclear war was under way. It took only a few minutes to reassure her that that was not what had happened, but years later I am still struck by the fact that the fear of nuclear attack was so much on her mind.

Surprisingly, not everyone is horrified at the prospect of a nuclear war or the erosion of the ozone layer to the point where our planet would become uninhabitable for human life. In the summer of 2007, journalist Alan Weisman wrote a book entitled *The World Without Us,* a scientific imagining of what would happen to the planet if all human beings disappeared, whether by plague, war, or other cause. How long would it take our buildings, our roads, our subway systems to wear down and crumble, and what would replace them? In his words, "How long would it take to recover lost ground and restore Eden to the way it must have gleamed and smelled before Adam?" Some human artifacts would begin to fall apart almost at once without human maintenance. Others, like bronze monuments and plastic bags, would last almost indefinitely. A foretaste of what a depopulated earth would look like would be the demilitarized zone separating North from South Korea. Because no humans have set foot there for decades, it has become a refuge for birds and wildlife that might otherwise have disappeared.

I got the impression from Weisman's book that he wrote it as an intellectual exercise, a speculation as to what the interaction between man's handiwork and nature might become if the human factor were taken out of the equation. But, although the book is interesting and gracefully written, I am less intrigued by the book itself and more by the question of why it became a best seller. I am not sure that people wanted to read it to learn how fast steel decomposes compared to concrete. I suspect people read it because they worry about the disappearance of the human race from the face of the earth. It may be the shadow of nuclear devastation; it may be the prospect of a devastating plague or global warming and the destruction of the environment. But suddenly the idea of a "world without us" seems less like science fiction and more like some future reality.

Some people seem to be looking forward to it. Weisman interviews Les Knight, founder of the Voluntary Human Extinction Movement, who believes that we are multiplying ourselves to the point where there won't be enough of the necessities of life to go around and life will be a constant war of survival. His solution: "Rather than face horrific resource wars and starvation . . . suppose we all agree to stop procreating." Just think: no more political quarrels over abortion, no more teenage gangs or juvenile delinquency (because there would be no juveniles), no more heartbreaking stories of children dying of cancer. "The last humans could enjoy their final sunsets peacefully, knowing that they have restored the planet as close as possible to the Garden of Eden."

And then there is the popularity of the Left Behind series of novels in which blessed souls are taken up to heaven, from which vantage point they can see everyone else suffer misery and death. Polls indicate that as many as 50 percent of Americans believe in the literal truth of the prophecies in the book of Revelation and anticipate the Rapture and/or the world-ending showdown at Armageddon.

I have two problems with the Rapture/Armageddon believers. First, I don't read the Bible as a guide to future events. The words of the biblical prophets may have been divinely inspired, but they were spoken by human beings to human beings living in their own day. There is an urgency to their words that makes it hard for me to believe that Isaiah or the author of Revelation was saying, Here is a vitally important message from God, but it won't be relevant for several thousand years. I don't believe that the future has been determined in advance. We are not moviegoers watching a film that has already been shot and edited while we sit there wondering how it will turn out. We are the actors and directors, not the audience. We get to determine the ending. If the world were to end, it would be because of human folly, not God's determination to make it happen.

Second, I find an unseemly delight on the part of too many people contemplating the suffering of all those who differ with them theologically and hoping to see them condemned to misery and punishment in their lifetime. I have always appreciated the Christianity that preached compassion for "even the least of these" more than the versions that led people to say, I'm going to Heaven and you're going to Hell because you don't believe what I believe. In the words of one Protestant minister, "I believe there is a Hell, but nobody lives there because God is too compassionate to consign any of His children to eternal damnation."

Then there are people who seem to be saying, as some people say about a diagnosis of serious illness, If it is going to happen, there is nothing I can do about it. So I'll just prepare myself for the inevitable.

Cormac McCarthy's prizewinning novel *The Road* portrays a post–nuclear holocaust America in which a few lonely survivors struggle to find food and shelter for another day or two before they too perish. One character in the book (and we must be careful not to assume that every character in a novel represents the opinion of the author) looks forward to the day when the last human being will die and put an end to the sordid tale of cruelty and suffering that is the story of humanity. For him, the death of the last human will mean the end of death and suffering. "When we are all gone at last then there'll be nobody here but death and his days will be numbered too. He'll be out in the road there with nothing to do and nobody to do it to."

In a similar vein, the distinguished theologian Jürgen Moltmann is less than horrified by the prospect of humanity's extinction. He was recently quoted as saying, "One should not speak about the end of the world if what one means is the end of our culture. If you are mankind-centered, it's a catastrophe; but if you are life-centered it is that while one life ends, another begins." In other words, when dinosaurs vanished from the world, it represented change but not tragedy. Another, higher form of life better adapted to live in the changing world emerged. We would be guilty of speciesism, thinking of human beings as qualitatively superior to other life-forms, if we were to deem the disappearance of humanity to be more of a tragedy than the extinction of the passenger pigeon or the possible disappearance of tigers or giant pandas.

At the risk of being guilty of speciesism, I would strenuously disagree with Moltmann. I would insist that the disappearance of the human race would be an incalculable tragedy. The prospect of human beings committing collective suicide, leaving a world without people, is just about the scariest scenario I can imagine. It breaks my heart to think that my grandchildren, and other people's grandchildren, might never get to grow up, marry, and know the fulfillment of parenthood. More than that, the disappearance of human beings from our planet would mean the disappearance of God.

In the 1992 novel *The Children of Men*, recently made into a movie, the British writer P. D. James imagines a world set twenty-five years in the future in which a mysterious plague has rendered all of humanity infertile. No babies are born anywhere; there is no one alive younger than twenty-five, and people trudge through their days with no hope of a future. James imagines a day, long after the last human being on earth has perished, when visitors from another far-off planet visit earth and explore the abandoned cathedrals of London. She writes, "Will they realize that this was once the greatest of man's temples to one of his many gods? Will they be curious about his nature, this deity who was worshipped with such pomp and splendor? . . . Or will their values and their thought processes be so alien to ours that nothing of awe or wonder will be able to touch them?"

The disappearance of humanity would mean the virtual disappearance of God from our earth. God would still exist in some abstract sense, but He would be completely absent from the world, perhaps from all worlds. The sun would still rise and set; the seasons would still change. But there would be no one to respond with a wordless prayer, no one to offer a blessing over the first ripe fruits of the harvest. It would be a world without love, without charity, without joy or forgiveness, a world in which no prayers of gratitude would be spoken and no wishes for a better future articulated, a world without any of the qualities we associate with God and made real on earth by the only creature described as fashioned in the image of God. When the old North Carolina storyteller Harry Golden was asked, "What would be the worst thing about a war that wiped out the entire human race?" he answered, "Nobody to hear the music of Mozart." The world would revert to what it was before the creation of Adam: "The earth was barren and nothing grew . . . for there was no human being to till the soil" (Genesis 2:5). Futurists who envision the restoration of the Garden of Eden once human beings vanish would do well to remember that God considered Eden incomplete until He put human beings there. Before that, there was order. Only after that could there be holiness, goodness, creativity, and love. In a sense, the question is not whether God will rescue humans from extinction but whether humans will rescue God from disappearing as a result of our self-destruction. If God craved a relationship with the only creatures that shared His sense of a moral dimension to life, if God felt His world was incomplete without human beings, who are we to disagree?

In theological discourse, the term "God" can be a subject for abstract discussion. But in the real world, in order for God to be real in this world, He has to be *somebody's* God. Remove human beings from the planet and you remove God. God would still exist in theory, in Heaven, but a world without people would be a world without God.

If we cannot turn to God to prevent us from committing suicide as a species, if we cannot persuade God that He needs us too much to let that happen, then what can we do? For one thing, we can work to elect governments that will stand up to wickedness but will not feel the need to prove their toughness by pushing the nuclear button. We can learn to admire firmness but reject posturing. I would like to believe that the American spirit is still guided by the ethos of the Western movies I admired when I was young, in which the hero takes no pleasure in having to use superior force. He employs the least amount of violence needed to prevent evil, and uses it reluctantly.

We can keep ourselves informed about large-scale threats to public health, monitoring the outbreaks of infectious disease in all parts of the globe and investing our resources in ways to confine, treat, and ultimately eliminate the diseases that kill people by the millions. We can commit ourselves to spending at least as much money on finding cures for disease and extending life as we spend on making ourselves sick in the first place.

We can take steps to slow the degradation of the environment before our planet becomes unlivable for reasons less apocalyptic than atomic war. We can insist that there are some things more important than maximizing profit and that among them are having clean air to breathe, safe water to drink, and food to eat that will not poison us. We can make it a priority to keep our planet livable to an extent that we have never done before, because never before has it seemed so urgent, and if we do, our reward will be that we and our descendants will continue to live on it.

If, despite our best efforts, mankind succeeds in destroying itself through nuclear holocaust, plague, or rendering the atmosphere unlivable, if the day comes when there are no humans left on earth, it will be lamentable, but at least we will be spared the problem of what to do about it. Yet what if the apocalypse resembles the Black Plague of fourteenth-century Europe more than the End of Days in the book of Revelation? What if some fraction of the human race survived, but we had to reinvent civilization, if we had to relearn how to grow food and transport it to the people who needed it, if we had to start all over again creating schools, factories, livelihoods? What if so many people perished and so few survived that life as we have known it would no longer be possible? What could we do then?

The prospect nearly overwhelms my imagination. I can hardly think how we would cope, where we would start, how decisions would be made. It would be more daunting than rebuilding the losing country after a horrific war. Then at least there would be other, less damaged countries to help, the way the United States helped Germany and Japan after World War II. But if every country was in that situation, who would be there to help?

It might be useful to realize that there is a helpful precedent, whether it is literally true or not, to which we can turn for guidance on how to go about rebuilding the world after human folly has destroyed it. The Bible offers us a case study in what to do and what not to do. Ten generations after the creation of the first human beings, mankind had become so utterly corrupt that God determined to wash the earth clean of them, sparing only the relatively virtuous Noah (described as "a righteous man *in his generation*" [Genesis 6:9; my emphasis]) with his wife, his sons, and his daughters-in-law. God sends a flood, and every living thing perishes except for the people and animals that were with Noah in the ark.

It takes a year for the waters that caused the flood to subside and the dry land to emerge. Noah, his family, and their menagerie leave the ark and confront a planet that needs to be rebuilt and repopulated virtually from scratch. What do they do first? Where does one start to rebuild a destroyed world? Noah does the wrong thing; his children get it right.

We read, "Noah was the first tiller of the soil. He planted a vineyard, drank of the wine and became drunk" (Genesis 9:20–21). I picture Noah as being so overwhelmed by the task he faced that he turned to drink. He may have felt overwhelmed by the magnitude of the challenge before him. He may have been grieving the death of friends and neighbors who would not be there to help him. He may have been paralyzed by "survivor guilt," wondering why he remained alive while so many others perished, perhaps even wishing that he had drowned with them so that he would not have to face this problem. Whatever the reason, he chose to avoid the problem rather than deal with it. It is a reaction I have seen in survivors of a tragedy, sole survivors of a crime or an automobile accident. They are too stunned to know what to do next. The memories of what happened may be too painful for them to recall. They may feel unworthy of having survived. I would try to tell them that going on with their lives is the only link to the ones who died. I would urge them to see their survival as a gift to be cherished rather than a burden to be borne. Like Noah, many survivors were unable to see it that way.

But Noah's children knew what to do. Their response to finding themselves alive on an empty planet was to have children of their own. Chapter 10 of Genesis consists of nothing more than a list of names, the descendants of Noah's sons. It is one of those notorious pages of "begats" that the casual reader of the Bible is tempted to skip, wondering why Scripture devotes an entire page to a collection of obscure names. But that list of "begats," families having children, is what saved the world. It made the difference between life continuing and life disappearing on our planet. To have a child is more than a biological event. It is a statement of faith in the future, a way of saying that you want there to be a future.

A few years ago, I was speaking at a conference on the West Coast where one of my fellow panelists was a prominent Orthodox rabbi whom I have long admired for his intellect, passion, and religious open-mindedness. It was the first time I had seen him since learning of the death of his son in an accident. During a break in the proceedings, I went up to him, offered my condolences, and said to him, "I know how the death of my son forced me to rethink what I believed about God. I know that you are Orthodox. How did your son's death affect your theology and that of your family?" He thought for a moment and replied, "How did it affect us theologically? The following year, each of my daughters had a baby."

I thought that was a wonderful answer. Choosing to conceive and bear a child *is* a theological statement, a way of saying that this is a world worth bringing a child into. It is an endorsement of the future, even by people who have found the past unacceptably painful. Children carry the promise of seeing and doing things differently than life-weary adults would. It is the best and bravest response I can think of, not only to pain and loss but to the uncertainty of a frightening future.

At the end of P. D. James's novel, the birth of a baby restores hope and optimism to a world that had been living without hope. Similarly, I believe that part of the appeal of the Christmas story to hundreds of millions of Christians is that it centers on the birth of a child at the darkest time of the year to a people suffering oppression under the despotic rule of the Roman Empire.

In Western Europe and some other parts of the world, women are not having as many babies. Demographers set "replacement level"—the number of offspring the average woman has to bear to keep the size of the population constant—at 2.1 children per adult woman, to allow for infant mortality, premature death, and childless women. But in a recent survey, European women were found to be having families well below replacement level, at a rate that leads demographers to calculate that the next generation will have one-third fewer people than in their parents' time. One writer refers to this trend as "Europe's demographic suicide."

Catholic theologian George Weigel, in his provocative book *The Cube and the Cathedral*, sees the decline as due to a lack of faith in the future caused by Europe's rejection of its religious past. He writes, "The failure to create a human future in the most elemental sense—by creating a successor generation—is surely an expression of a broader failure: a failure of self-confidence. That broader failure is no less surely tied to a collapse of faith in the God of the Bible." Europeans, Weigel suggests, are embarrassed by religion, embarrassed by any reference to Europe's Christian heritage, perhaps because of times when an excess of religious zeal or a paucity of religious courage led to religion's involvement in outright wickedness, from the Inquisition to racial and religious persecution to complicity in the Holocaust. Or perhaps these young families reject religion because religion keeps telling them not to do things they would like to do.

For Weigel, this is tragic. It threatens the survival of Western civilization, which he sees as our main bulwark against barbarism. We dare not reject the past; the past contains the wisdom we need to deal with the future.

I would differ with Weigel's analysis. I see the decline in fertility stemming not from a rejection of the past but from a rejection of the future, not a flight from Europe's religious roots but a lack of faith in humanity's ability to create a world fit to raise children in. People are afraid to see their children grow up in a world of cruelty and conflict, along with the temptation of addictive drugs and shortages of the essentials of life.

Perhaps the greatest challenge to our ability to believe in the future enough to invest in it came in the wake of the Depression and the Second World War, a sixteen-year-long ordeal that tested the faith of everyone who lived through it. When the war ended, leaving millions of people dead and much of Europe and Asia in ruins, some people responded as Noah did after the Flood, so disgusted by what they had seen of human behavior at its most depraved, so overwhelmed by the challenge of putting the world back together again, that they gave up. They let the past color their view of the future and feared a future that would be more of the same—more war, more killing, more enmity. Is it only a coincidence that the steepest declines in population today are taking place in Western Europe and Japan, countries that suffered most during World War II, enduring Nazi occupation, the Holocaust, and the dropping of two atomic bombs? A generation or two later, might some people be saying, Why should I bring a child into a world where things like that happened and could well happen again?

But not everyone responded that way. American GIs returning from the horrors of war in Europe and the Pacific gave rise to the Baby Boom, the largest cohort of births in human history. Like the children of Noah, it was as if they could hardly wait to have families to repopulate a world short of people. Jewish survivors of the Holocaust, almost all of whom had seen loved ones murdered, found their way to Israel and, in the face of continuing threats and hatred, chose to affirm life and hope. They dared to marry and have new children to replace the people they had lost. These people responded to a past of bloodshed and destruction not by giving up on the future of the human race but by saying, This is what we fought and suffered for; this is what we survived to be able to do, to raise our families in peace and hope. They may even have been thinking that there would be less reason to fear the future and more reason for hope if there were more people with their values in the world.

For human beings as for no other creature, the act of bringing a child into this world is more than a biological event. It affirms our belief that the past is worth passing on to the future, and that the future, the world that will be here after we are gone, is worth investing our care in. *Boston Globe* columnist Jeff Jacoby has written, "A world without children will be a poorer world—grayer, lonelier, less creative, less confident. Children are a great blessing, but it may take their disappearance for the world to remember why." Is that enough to ensure the survival of the human race on our planet? Obviously not. But it is a start, an essential start, without which nothing else will matter. It is, in the familiar phrase of classes in logic, "necessary but not sufficient." Clearly, more will need to be done to rebuild a destroyed world than simply having families, but having families makes all the rest worth doing. We testify to our belief in a future by bearing children and by doing things today that imply a future.

Even people who are well beyond the age of bearing children can make a viable human future more likely by doing things today that will bear fruit long after they are no longer around to see them. They can advocate for better schools, strive to eliminate diseases, work to limit the using up of natural resources so that future generations will not lack them. We sometimes speak colloquially of people who "use things up as if there were no tomorrow." But if too many people do that, there may well be no tomorrow.

There is a story in the Talmud about an old man who planted a tree that would not bear fruit for many years, by which time he would no longer be around to enjoy it. He explained, I was not born into a world without fruit trees. As my ancestors planted trees for me, I plant for the generations to come. It was an act in the spirit of the sons of Noah, a way of saying, The world will be around at least two or three generations down the road, and this is my gift to those who will be alive then. If I don't do something like this today, I am afraid that my children will grow up in a barren, unlivable world.

Maybe there is nothing we can do that will guarantee the survival of the human race. Maybe there are threats to our survival, natural or human, beyond our control. But there are things we can do to make it more likely that the human race will survive, and perhaps the most important one is to do what the children of Noah did and what the old man with his tree did: Act on the assumption that there will be a future, and you make that future more likely. Withhold your investment in the future because you are afraid there may not be one, and you make that future less likely. We would be like people who stop maintaining their homes because they plan to move, and before long, the house begins to fall apart.

I once heard Elie Wiesel, Holocaust survivor and recipient of the Nobel Peace Prize, speak about the biblical story of Adam and Eve. He reminded us that they had had two children, Cain and Abel. One of their sons killed the other and fled, and they never saw him again. Suddenly, they who had had so much had nothing. How did they respond? They had more sons and daughters. Wiesel went on to say—and everyone in the audience knew that he was talking not about two mythical biblical figures but about himself and his generation—that the greatness of Adam and Eve was not just that they were the first, that they represented the beginning of the human race, but that when everything they had was taken from them, when that which they feared most had come to pass, they had the courage to begin again. To begin something new, he said, is a wondrous thing. But to lose everything and be able to begin over again is nothing less than a miracle.

I think back to that young woman in the Copenhagen synagogue, to the underlying fear that led to her question as to whether God would let humanity destroy itself. I realize today that what I should have told her was that she was asking the wrong question. The destruction of humanity will never be an act of God. The real questions are, first, will human beings realize the awesome magnitude of their power to do harm on a scale hitherto unimagined, and will their inability to control their rage lead them to let destruction loose on our world? And second, if, God forbid, that were to happen and only a saving remnant was left behind, would God give them the wisdom and the courage He gave the children of Noah, to be inspired by a vision of a world rebuilt, a world worth living in and

CONQUERING FEAR

bringing children into? And would the survivors do what needs to be done to give birth to such a world?

The prophet Habakkuk lived in a time of catastrophe. He saw his homeland overrun and God's Temple in Jerusalem destroyed by the Babylonian army. All around him, people's vision of the future was colored more by fear than by hope. But he was nevertheless able to look beyond that time of devastation and see a future worth working for. He defined the essence of faith in just seven words (three words in the original Hebrew): "the righteous shall live by his faith" (Habakkuk 2:4). I would paraphrase his statement to mean: The righteous person translates his faith into life. He does not fear the future. He testifies to his faith that this is a world we can live in, despite what we have gone through, not only by his own life but by generating the lives that will one day create that future world.

6

*

Loss of Job, Loss of Love

THE FEAR OF REJECTION

What I fear most is that I am not loved.

BENNETT CERF

The quotation that appears above comes from a book by Robert Ball entitled *Being With*. It was uttered on a television program some years ago in which several prominent people were asked what they were most afraid of. The answers included fear of cancer, fear of nuclear war, fear of violent crime. When the question was put to Bennett Cerf, a founding editor of Random House and a prominent TV personality of the 1960s and 1970s, he answered with the words in this chapter's epigraph. I suspect a lot of people share that fear.

An unforgettable story from the Holocaust tells of a group of Jewish inmates in a Nazi concentration camp. It was the first night of Hanukkah, the winter holiday that recalls the victory of the weak over the powerful and the few over the many in the second century B.C.E. Hanukkah always falls at the darkest time of the year, and Jews mark it by lighting candles against the cold and dark. Holiday celebrations were forbidden in the camp, but one man saved a bit of the bread from his evening meal, dipped it in grease from his dinner bowl, fashioned it into an impromptu candle, said the appropriate prayer, and lit the bread. His son said to him, "Father, that was food you burned. We have so little of it. Wouldn't we have been better off eating it?" The father replied, "My son, people can live for a week without food, but they cannot live for one day without hope."

I would expand the father's words to include the recognition that, as for Bennett Cerf, living for long without love is something a great many people find unbearable. The love I have in mind is not limited to romantic or physical love. We desperately need the reassurance that we are cherished, that someone somewhere thinks we are special, and if we sense that we don't have it or may be losing it, we will do desperate things to get it and hold on to it. William James once wrote, "No more fiendish punishment could be devised . . . than that one should be turned loose in society and remain absolutely unnoticed by all the members thereof."

When things are going well, we can get that feeling of being cherished from our intimate partners, and when we start to worry that it may be slipping away, we respond strongly, sometimes violently. How do we understand the phenomenon of husbands and wives murdering their spouses, killing someone they once thought they loved more than anyone in the world? It will almost always be because one is afraid of losing the other's love or because the marriage partner stands in the way of finding a new and more satisfying love. I remember the thirty-five-year-old woman who sat across from me in my study one day and told me, "When we were first married, my husband made me feel special. He made me feel that I was the most important thing in his life. I tried so hard to be a good wife and mother, but I don't get that feeling of being special from him anymore."

We can get that feeling of being appreciated for being the special person we are from our family and friends, and—it may surprise you to know—from our work. Obviously, people work primarily to earn money, to pay their bills and support their families. But we also work at our jobs for the recognition that we are doing something valuable and that others appreciate us for it. That is why so many people, from lottery winners to sixty-year-old millionaires, keep on working even when there is no economic reason to do so. For employers and managers, giving workers the feeling that their contributions are appreciated is not only good manners; it is good business. The worker who feels recognized and appreciated is more likely to try harder, less likely to take days off for sick leave, and more resistant to offers from other companies, while the worker who does not get that psychological reward along with his paycheck is more likely to resent his job and give it less than his total commitment. I remember meeting Ken Blanchard, author of the One-Minute Manager series of books, and being impressed by his commitment to humanizing the employer-employee relationship as a matter of morality as well as an economic guideline. At the heart of his teaching is the simple and cost-free recommendation that we compliment people for what they are doing well instead of only pointing out what they are doing wrong. Even the most menial job will be seen as more rewarding when that happens.

Love and work. They don't seem to belong in the same sentence, let alone in the same discussion, an examination of the parts of our lives whose possible loss terrifies us. But, in fact,

they are the two primary sources of the emotional nourish-
ment we need to feel cherished and to live our lives with
enthusiasm and confidence. That is why the fear of rejection,
the prospect of losing our job or of no longer feeling loved, is
perhaps the most shattering of all fears. How often have we
read of rejected lovers choosing one of the two paths people
can take to deal with pain, turning it inward and becoming
depressed or turning it outward and acting violently against
the one who rejected them or against the person who was chosen instead of them? They will harass, stalk, and even threaten
to kill someone they once believed they loved. Sometimes the
rejected lover will combine the anger against oneself and the
anger against the one who rejected him or her in an act of self-
destruction. I remember a funeral at which I had to officiate
during my first year at my current congregation. A young man
had left his job and broken with his family for the love of a
woman whom his family found unsuitable. Her religion, her
reputation, and her educational background were not what
they were hoping for in a partner for their son. After a few
months, the woman told him that it wasn't working out and
she didn't want to see him anymore. He cried, pleaded, then
told her he understood and left. An hour later, he reappeared
in front of her home, calling her name. When she came to the
window, he shot and killed himself while she watched helplessly, ending a life that had become unbearable without love.

The prospect of losing one's job, as so many people have
learned in recent months, can generate feelings of pain and
loss, feelings of anger turned inward or anger turned outward,
in part because of the loss of income but also because of the
implicit message that one is of no use to the company. A fifty-
five-year-old business executive shared with me his fear that his

job would be eliminated following his company's merger with a larger firm. I asked him what concerned him more, the loss of income or the psychological loss of the feeling of being needed. He told me, "Forty percent the money, sixty percent the message that they don't need me anymore." (Had he been several years younger, the percentages might well have been reversed.)

How often have you read an account of a man being fired from his job, going home to get a gun, then returning to his workplace and shooting at the people who fired him and at his former colleagues who still had their jobs? How often have you read of a high school student so enraged at being assigned to the "loser" category, while the brains, the athletes, and the cheerleaders got all the attention, to the point that he lashes out in an orgy of killing? Having suffered the punishment William James called "the most fiendish," he sees any fate as being better than the one he finds himself living.

Love and work are the two sources of emotional reassurance whose loss we fear so much that we will go without food or sleep to gain and hold on to them. They seem to be such different things, but they have been linked in two important speeches, uttered thousands of years apart.

In chapter 3 of Genesis, God confronts Adam and Eve after they have eaten from the Tree of the Knowledge of Good and Evil, something He had warned them not to do. I don't see God's words to Adam and Eve as a curse and a punishment but rather a matter of alerting them to how much more complicated their lives will now be, because they are human and not mere animals. And what does God speak to them about in His warnings? He speaks to them about love and work.

God says to Eve, "In pain shall you bring forth children, yet your urge shall be for your husband" (Genesis 3:16). That is, animals mate, bear their young, and after a brief interval, send them out on their own. Humans worry endlessly over issues of sexuality, attractiveness, courtship, marriage, fidelity, and parenthood. I understand the reference to the pain of bearing children as referring not only to the process of giving birth but to the anguish parents feel when children don't turn out as they hoped they would. Eve, who named her first child Cain, meaning "possession," will see him leave home as a fugitive and never return.

And yet, who among us would prefer to bear and raise children the way animals do, with none of the pleasure, albeit none of the anguish, that comes with parenthood? Raising a child, being disappointed by aspects of that child's behavior and limitations, worrying about the child as he grows up, and one day setting the child free to be his own person and find his own way in life will be among the most painful things we will ever have to do, but think of how much would be missing from our lives without all that.

And to Adam, God says, "By the sweat of your brow shall you get bread to eat" (Genesis 3:19). Animals go out in search of food, and their instincts direct them as to what to eat and where to find it. But human beings have to choose a career, prepare for it, compete for jobs, earn money, and worry about keeping the job they have. Animals recognize feelings of hunger and the urge to mate and reproduce, but words like "love" and "work" are meaningless to them. To human beings, these words represent the sources of the greatest satisfaction we will ever know and the most desperate fears we will ever experience. They represent what we crave more than anything else and what we fear losing or not having more than anything else.

"To love and to work." Those two words come together

again in Sigmund Freud's famous answer to the question of what a well-adjusted person should be able to do well: love, the achievement of intimacy with another person, the sense of being cherished for who you are; and work, the experience of competence, being admired for what you can do. If we need them for our well-being, how can we cope with the prospect of losing them?

First, please realize that *sometimes smart people make mistakes*. When you think about it, that should be obvious. If you want proof, I can give it to you in two words: "New Coke." (Or if you are of my generation, one word will do: "Edsel.") Talented and successful business leaders thought long and hard and came up with a product they were sure people would rush out to buy, only to have people utterly reject it. Professional football teams spend millions of dollars scouting college prospects, yet half of their first-round draft picks never have successful professional careers. If you interviewed for a job that you thought you would be perfect for and one that would be perfect for you, but the company chose someone else, console yourself with the thought that they may have made a wrong decision, even if you are the one who has to suffer as a result. If the rejection came in a romantic situation rather than a professional one, if the man of your dreams settled his affections on someone else, console yourself with the thought that, if he preferred large breasts to a sensitive soul, why would you want to be married to a jerk like that in the first place? Yes, it can hurt terribly to be rejected. It can leave you questioning your future and your own worth, but it may have been the result of someone else's limitations, not yours. Sometimes you deserved to be chosen and cherished, but other people's blindness kept that from happening.

Second, *sometimes smart people get it right even if we don't like the result.* The fact that someone else was hired for a job instead of you need not be seen as a rejection of you as a person. It may mean that your skills were not what the interviewer was looking for or what the job required, or that, impressive as you may have been, someone who was more impressive applied for the same job that you coveted.

Once, early in my tenure at my Massachusetts synagogue, I applied for the position of rabbi at a large congregation in another state. My children were at an age when changing schools and leaving friends would not be as much of an issue as it would when they were older. The other synagogue offered a larger staff and membership, a much higher salary, and was more conveniently located to schools and medical care. The congregation considered my application seriously but ultimately chose someone else. I was their second choice among the dozen or so candidates who applied. I was deeply disappointed. In the ensuing years, I would console myself with the thought that, every time one of my books made the best-seller list and every time I appeared on national television, the leaders of that congregation would think, He could have been ours. (I had the same thoughts about some old girlfriends.) Then I met and became friendly with the colleague whom they chose instead of me, and he told me about some of the problems he was having there. The leadership included some very successful businessmen who were not accustomed to having "hired help" disagree with them. The membership was evenly divided between people who threatened to resign if things changed too rapidly and people who threatened to resign if they changed too slowly. He was able to hold things together by postponing some changes, most involving the role of women in services, changes I might have been more eager to implement at once. I was left to ponder the thought that, hurtful as it was for me to be rejected, hard as it may have been for me to admit that someone else was better suited than I was for a job I coveted, the congregation may actually have been right. I may not have been the best candidate for the job.

Thomas Moore, who has written so many perceptive books about the nurturing of our souls, tells the story in one of his recent books about a colleague on the faculty of the college where Moore worked who was denied tenure and could not accept the judgment of the committee. He complained; he petitioned for reconsideration; he threatened legal action. He simply could not face the fact that he was not cut out to be a university professor. He could not imagine himself in any other line of work. Moore himself would be denied tenure at the same institution a few years later and would respond differently. He took the rejection as a sign for him to move on to another line of work. Once he got over the pain of having been rejected, he learned to be grateful to the committee for extracting him from a job he was not truly suited for and pointing him in a more fulfilling direction.

I once went to New York to meet with a woman who was handling a professional matter for me. When I sat down with her, I saw right away that her mind was elsewhere. She told me that she had just had to fire her administrative assistant after only a few months on the job because the person had turned out to be totally unsuitable for what was needed. The employee had cried and pleaded, and her boss was clearly feeling guilty for having caused her such distress. To ease her guilt, I told her that in my experience, you never do people a favor by keeping them in a position that is not right for them. It is like wearing a suit or dress that is too tight for you. The longer you try to do it, the more uncomfortable you feel. Sometimes it is a painful act of kindness to remove someone from a situation like that.

Because the woman I was talking to had a thorough religious education, I reminded her of the story of King Saul in the Bible. He was the first king of Israel, appointed to provide permanent leadership in place of the unreliable dependence on charismatic judge-leaders. But it soon became clear that it was too big a job for him. Too proud and stubborn to step aside (as Robert Frost suggests in one of his poems, it is hard to turn down the opportunity to be a king), he grew increasingly paranoid, seeing enemies everywhere, attacking people close to him, and ultimately descending into self-destructive madness. He might have been better off had someone been able to offer him a face-saving way to be relieved of the responsibility.

In much the same way, the person who rejects you in a personal relationship, whether by not pursuing a courtship or by initiating a divorce, might understand you better than you understand yourself and might see you more clearly than you see yourself. I can recall one young man who broke off his engagement after the ring had been bought, the hall had been rented, and the invitations printed. I met with him and his fiancée to see if this was just a normal case of prewedding jitters, but the young man persisted in his feeling that something about the impending marriage bothered him, and he wasn't ready to get married. After an understandable time of tears and anger, the rejected fiancée was able to say to me, "Better now than after years of marriage and children."

You may have your reasons for not wanting to recognize that things are not working out, but it may be more obvious to your partner. To your implicit, unspoken message of If you love me, that will solve all of my problems, the other person's implicit, unspoken answer is Yes, but solving your problems is not my primary purpose in life. You'll have to solve some of them yourself.

Third and most important of all: *Do not ever let your opinion of yourself be shaped by someone else's opinion of you.* If an employer tells you that you are incompetent, if he sends you out the door with the benediction "You will never amount to anything," you don't have to believe him or fear that he is right. He may be trying to ease his own guilt at having to terminate you or to cover his mistake in hiring you in the first place, or he may just be a poor judge of talent. Even if you were not good at that particular job, it doesn't mean that you are destined to be a hopeless failure. You may learn to be good at it, or you may find another line of work at which you can excel. When I was in college, I tried to earn some pocket money by teaching Sunday school at a nearby synagogue. I was a terrible teacher back then, unable to control the class or to make the material interesting. It was an act of mercy to me and to the children when I was told at year's end that I would not be invited back. But I didn't like being an unsuccessful teacher. In future opportunities, I worked harder to prepare and, before long, I was good at it. Years later, after I had become a well-known author and sought-after public speaker, that congregation invited me back to speak. I accepted their invitation at a greatly reduced fee, feeling that I owed them one. Rather than concluding that I would never be good at something, I learned to be better at it.

Should a lover break off a relationship by telling you that you are cold and selfish and that no one will ever love you, he may be projecting his own problems onto you, or he may simply be looking for a way to end the relationship without having to take responsibility for ending it. It will be a painful message for you to hear from someone you care about, but it doesn't mean that it is true. And no one has the right to make you feel like a failure by dumping their problems on you.

One word of caution: There is an old proverb that says, "If one person calls you a donkey, ignore him. If two or three people do, buy yourself a saddle." You can ignore one person's rejection as stemming from his problems more than yours, but if you keep getting the same message time after time, there might be a reason to take it seriously.

You have experienced rejection, been fired from a job, spurned by a potential marriage partner, and you fear that the same thing may happen again. How do you cope? You might begin by remembering the enduring truth taught by Viktor Frankl in his book *Man's Search for Meaning:* You cannot control what other people do to you, but you can always control how you respond to what they do. You can make the rejection serve as a spur to increased competence and self-awareness. The next crucial step would be to realize that you will do a better job of getting over the rejection if you don't have to do it alone. Don't hide what happened to you out of a sense of embarrassment. Reach out to friends and let them help you. Let them reassure you that you are in fact a person worth cherishing.

When I was rejected for what I thought would be my dream job, the congregation I wrote about earlier, I should have had no reason to think it was the end of the world. I still had a good job. I had my health. I had my family. But the rejection hurt deeply. It made me question how good I really was at what I did and whether I would ever get a better job than the one I held at the time. Fortunately, I had a friend who had been through a similar experience and knew what I needed. He and his wife took my wife and me out for dinner at a nice restaurant. We had a good meal and more wine than we would ordinarily drink. We laughed; we shared stories about the rabbinate and about synagogue leaders. And it worked. It worked not because of anything anyone said or did that night but because of the unspoken message our friends delivered: You're good, you're capable, and you are someone we care about.

In the 1970s, the federal government cut back sharply on funding for weapons systems, including several that were being developed in laboratories along Boston's Route 128. In the course of a few months, thousands of highly skilled, well-paid engineers lost their jobs. Churches and synagogues in the area were overwhelmed with formerly affluent families asking for help to pay their mortgages and their school tuition bills. I especially remember one congregant who was one of the last to be let go because he was so good at what he did, developing ceramic components for weapons that would have to withstand high temperatures. When he was finally told to leave his job, he realized that the thing he was really good at was something no one needed any longer, and at his age, in his mid-fifties, he thought he was probably too old to learn a new specialty. He became deeply depressed, feeling worthless, waking up every morning with no place to go and nothing challenging to do. His marriage fell apart. Despite his intelligence and his employment history, he had no energy to even think about retraining for another line of work. He would come to my office every week and just sit for an hour and pour out his sense of helplessness and his doubts about his worth. Despite all his awards, his patents, his reputation, how good could he really be if no one was willing to hire him? I would listen and, remembering what my friend had done for me years before, I would assure him that he was a good man and a good engineer, capable of being a good husband, father, and wage earner despite what he was temporarily going through. Finally, someone in the community was able to give him the one thing I could not. He found a job for him, and before long, he was his old funny, cantankerous self again. I didn't solve his problem, but I like to think that the time I spent listening to him made his problem easier to bear until circumstances changed for the better.

In the last thirty-five years, the plague of job eliminations that affected New England and California in the 1970s has spread to almost every sector of the economy. People have always had to change jobs and look for work for one reason or another. Companies go out of business due to ineffective management or changing conditions. But in recent years, we have become familiar with terms like "downsizing" and "outsourcing." The tacit agreement between employer and employee that people would be retained in their jobs unless they were guilty of gross incompetence or dishonesty or the company was in dire financial straits was no longer holding. Thirty-five years ago, when I would teach a class on religious values and business ethics, it was the unanimous position of the businessmen in the class that the most difficult ethical decision they ever had to make was not whether or not to do something dishonest but whether to let a longtime, hardworking employee go, either because he could no longer do his job or because the company's financial situation left them no alternative. One middle manager told me that he had been unable to sleep the night before he had to tell one-third of his department that they would be let go because the company had lost a large contract. I told him I understood that he had no choice and that the firing without the loss of sleep or the loss of sleep without the firing—had he, out of pity, kept the employees in their jobs, damaging the company financially—would have been a violation of his ethical obligations.

But by the dawn of the twenty-first century, things had changed. Now business executives are rewarded not for making a profit but for maximizing profits. Fire one-tenth of your workforce, make everyone else work 10 percent harder to keep their jobs, get more production at less expense, see the stock price of the company rise, and you will be richly rewarded for it. But what happens to the self-esteem of the person who is let go even though he has been doing his job faithfully? What happens to his sense of the world as a fair place where you are recognized and rewarded for what you do? Will these people be able to devote themselves to another job with the same level of commitment, or will they have learned the lesson that loyalty in the workplace is a one-way street? Will they conclude that it is a mistake to give your heart and soul to the company that employs you? Will workers be less reliable, less creative, and care less about the quality of their work? Will they learn to fear a future marked by heartless exploitation?

New York Times business reporter Louis Uchitelle, in his book *The Disposable American*, describes what happens when one state uses the attraction of tax breaks and a less expensive workforce to persuade a company to close its plant in another state and relocate. If the workers left behind cannot easily find new jobs, they are blamed for lacking the flexibility to find employment. They blame themselves for their plight.

Uchitelle quotes an organizational psychologist on how the impact of being laid off "limits all kinds of other activities, for example, the ability to form emotional bonds or to try new things." Even interviewing for another job can be daunting. If you feel bad about yourself, you don't want to risk another rejection or another failure.

It can be a terrifying experience to lose your job. It hurts you financially and erodes your self-confidence just when you most need a financial cushion and a healthy sense of self-confidence to deal with your plight. What can you do when it happens? There are some things you probably should have been doing before you were let go at work, chief among them saving money on a regular basis. When we realize how fragile the economy can be, it makes sense to live just below our means rather than to spend every dollar we earn with the confidence that the money will never stop flowing in. Financial advisers like to say, "Pay yourself first." That is, save money out of every paycheck even if that means one less restaurant meal or waiting longer between major purchases.

The advice columnists differ as to whether you should start looking for a new job right away or take some time to let the wound heal and enjoy downtime with your family. Being between jobs can let you experience life as a person, as a husband or wife, a father or mother, rather than as a provider. The answer will probably depend on whether you have the financial cushion to let you pay your bills and put food on the table while you are between jobs. You might use that time to ask yourself how satisfied you were in your previous position and whether you want to find another one like it. If you feel it is what you were meant to do with your life, that commitment may come through in an interview and tip the scales in your favor. But you might want to use your involuntary downtime to ask yourself if there is something else you might want to do, even if it means learning a new skill or a new language or becoming more computer literate. You may end up looking back at being fired as the best thing that could have happened to you.

If things don't work out, if you and your spouse have to resign yourself to a lower standard of living, don't let that make you feel like a failure. Don't compare yourself with your neighbors or even with your former lifestyle. You will probably still be living better than most people throughout history.

Never forget: Though society tends to define people on the basis of what they earn, you don't have to go along with that. You are free to define yourself as a good human being, a good family member, a good friend and neighbor. As the author of the biblical book Ecclesiastes puts it, "A good name is worth more than precious ointment" (Ecclesiastes 7:1).

What shall we say about a society that wounds souls and destroys families in order to maximize shareholder value? Americans seem to be of two minds on the subject. On the one hand, they feel it is wrong for a company to lay off capable American workers only because the work can be done more cheaply overseas. They feel compassion for their unemployed, downsized neighbors. But these same people cherish the low prices at Wal-Mart, never connecting them to the lower costs of manufacturing in Asia rather than in the town next door.

Cultural critic Louis Menand, taking issue with economists who fault people for valuing sentiment over efficiency, argues that most people do not think like economists. He writes, "Most people, even if you explained to them what the economically rational choice was, would be reluctant to make it, because they value other things . . . They would rather feel good about themselves than maximize (even legitimately) their profit." They are left uncomfortable by the cheerful assertion of some economists that "after technology throws people out of work, they have an incentive to find a new use for their talents." As medical economist Rashi Fein puts it: "We live in a society, not just an economy."

If you think that arming people against the fear of losing their jobs is daunting, how would you help people get over the fear of losing another person's love? It is not by chance that no ancient myth tells of magic instruments designed to keep people employed (though several tales tell of becoming wealthy without working for it), but many tell of the quest for a love potion. As we have noted, the need for love, the sense of loss when we are deprived of it, is so overwhelming that for many people, life itself loses all savor without it. It is more than a craving for sex, for a warm body to sleep next to. It is the need to know that you are cherished, that someone thinks you are special. It is the antidote to the curse that William James described at the beginning of this chapter, the feeling of having to go through life unrecognized and unappreciated. That is why people will do desperate things for love, and even more desperate things to fend off the threat of its loss.

How then does one heal a broken heart? When the poet Tennyson wrote " 'Tis better to have loved and lost than never to have loved at all," I imagine he meant that the feeling of being in love is such an exhilarating one that a person would not want to go through life without experiencing it, even if it did not last. But I find another level of meaning in his words. Isn't it true that it is by loving and losing, by rejecting and being rejected, that we ultimately find the person we are most suited to share a life of love with?

When I was promoting a previous book of mine, one interviewer asked me, "Wouldn't we be happier if we never had to face disappointment?" I told him, "I don't think so. Would you really want to be married today to the first girl you ever had a crush on? Yes, it's a sad thing to say good-bye to someone you cared about, and it can be really painful to be told by someone you dreamed of sharing a life with that 'It's not working out.' But that is how you find out who you are. You try on one identity, one combination after another until you find the one that fits just right."

We find the salve to heal a broken heart in the same place we find the balm to get over losing our job. We may have to acknowledge that the man or woman we thought was so perfect had flaws that would ultimately have led to mutual unhappiness. (People who appear to be perfect tend to have large egos and often have an exaggerated sense of entitlement.) Or we may have to acknowledge that the person we thought was so wise and so wonderful may have been wise enough to realize that the two of you were not really right for each other, not necessarily because there was something lacking in you but because there was something about the combination of the two of you that didn't quite fit.

What do you do then? First, you grieve. Don't be in too much of a hurry to replace the person who abandoned you, and don't dismiss the deep feelings you may have had for that person. Don't pretend you never cared. Your friends are not doing you a favor when they say to you, "I never liked him anyway. I don't know what you ever saw in him." You had something precious, something meaningful for a while. Give yourself time to savor the memory and then deposit it in your memory bank.

In addition, the experience of having been rejected, whether for a job or for a lasting personal relationship, teaches us a very valuable lesson: We are strong enough to survive being rejected. A broken heart is like a broken leg, and a bruised ego is like a bruised arm. We hurt but we heal. The worst lesson one might come away with would be the fear of trying again for fear of being hurt again. We can paraphrase Tennyson to warn us that it is worse to be afraid of loving lest you lose than it is to love and lose. The person who is afraid to try guarantees that he or she will not gain the prize. Helen Keller once wrote, "Security is mostly a superstition. It does not exist in nature, nor do the children of men as a whole experience it. . . . Life is either a daring adventure or nothing."

This brings us to one last aspect of our fear of rejection. We are often afraid to try because we don't trust ourselves to get over the disappointment of failing. Even worse, we are afraid of what other people will think of us if we fail. Ours is a culture that worships winners, even if they cheat to win, and scorns losers despite their admirable qualities. President Barack Obama remembers how he felt the first time he ran for public office. "There is . . . an emotion that, after the giddiness of your official announcement as a candidate, rapidly locks you in its grip and doesn't release you until after Election Day. That emotion is fear. Not just fear of losing—although that is bad enough—but fear of total, complete humiliation."

I remember once saying to a member of my congregation

who was thinking of running for a position in local government, "Why don't you try it? I think you'd be good for the town. But even if you run and lose, it's the town's loss, and you'll be exactly where you are now." She told me, "No, it would be different. Today I don't know if my neighbors think well enough of me to entrust me with this responsibility. If I run and lose, I'll know that they don't." I replied, "I'm not sure that would be the case. First of all, you might win. But even if you lose, they might admire you for wanting to serve the community, maybe even for being willing to do something they are reluctant to do. They might have voted for the other guy because they know him better, not because they like you less. Having the confidence in yourself to try something and risk failure, trusting in your own power of resilience, says something about you that a lot of people, many of them lacking that self-confidence, will admire."

Rejection hurts, failure hurts—whether it is in an election, a job, or a romantic relationship. It hurts because it represents someone, or several people, saying, I don't need you. There is nothing special about you that I can't find elsewhere. The cure for the pain of rejection is having friends who will say to you, No, we need you. We recognize the special qualities in you that make you such a good friend. Let us supply the caring that will bind up your wounds.

Don't let the fear of rejection scare you into not even trying and thereby rob you of the possibility of either winning or else gaining the wisdom that will help you win the next time. Rejection hurts, but the person who has loved and lost and lived to love again, the person who has lost a job and suffered through sleepless nights haunted by the fear that he might never find another one, yet who ultimately learns that his family loves him not only for being a good provider but loves him all the more and hurts for him when he hurts, that person (and that includes most of us) has been vaccinated against the fear of rejection. Having had a case of it and recovered, those people may well now be immune to the fear of rejection that hovers over their unscarred neighbors. They will have learned something about how strong, how resilient, and how cherished they are, and whatever may happen to them tomorrow, they will not be afraid.

7

Can Seventy Be the New Fifty?

THE FEAR OF GROWING OLD

> The cruel looking-glass that will never show a lass
> As comely or as kindly or as young as what she was!
>
> RUDYARD KIPLING, "The Looking-Glass"

W hen I was a child, I always knew how old I was, and
I could hardly wait to be older. I knew how many
months, how many days stood between me and my next birth-
day. To me, being older meant that I would have more privi-
leges, more freedom. I would be taken more seriously. I would
feel complimented if some adult mistook me for being older
than I was and offended if someone looked at me and assumed
I was younger.

Then there came a point in my life, as happens to virtually
everyone, varying from person to person and from occupation
to occupation, when the prospect of turning a year older began
to fill me with dismay. Athletes may dread turning thirty, while
a senator may feel he is reaching his prime at sixty-five. Suddenly, being taken for younger than we are becomes a compliment, and we are offended when someone assumes we are
older than the calendar would testify.

What changes? It may be that we do not look forward to

becoming more like older people. We fear the loss of physical attractiveness. We are apprehensive that our bodies will begin to slow down and become more vulnerable to serious disease. And we worry that in a world in which people are valued for being attractive and productive, as we grow older people will automatically take us less seriously, no matter what we do.

Most of us will first experience the impact of growing older in our appearance. As Kipling understood, you will look into the mirror and realize that, however young you may think yourself to be, to the world you are beginning to look older. One day, the face looking back at us is no longer our face as we have always thought of it but more like our mother's or father's face as we remember them. Men and women alike are susceptible to the shock of looking older, but women are probably more vulnerable because society places more emphasis on a woman's appearance than on a man's. Unattractive middle-aged men, if they are successful enough, can be deemed "interesting" or "showing a lot of character in their face" more readily than women of the same age. (As one cynic put it, it's remarkable how much taller a man looks when he stands on his wallet.) But a female friend once told me, "It used to bother me when men stared at me when I walked by. Now it bothers me when they don't."

There is no question that being attractive is an advantage in life. Better-looking people are more likely to be hired, not only for positions where appearance is relevant but even where it should make no difference. In experiments, college students were given photos and biographical sketches of individuals and asked to guess how they would perform in various situations. Some of the subjects were strikingly good-looking while others were doctored to look unattractive; the biographical details were balanced equally. Invariably, the students guessed that the better-looking candidates would be brighter, more imaginative, and better coworkers. I have long suspected that elections are decided at least in part on the basis of which candidate's face we would rather see on our television screens every day for the next several years.

If thinking of yourself as good-looking is an important part of your self-image and if society's image of attractiveness tilts younger as you grow older, you will understandably be upset, perhaps even verging on panic, when the "cruel looking-glass" reflects signs of age back at you.

Men as well as women are vulnerable to these fears. One evening after I had lectured at a Florida synagogue, my wife and I were taken to dinner by the rabbi and the past president of the congregation and their wives. The subject of my talk had been how we find the resources to cope with the misfortunes in our lives, and over dinner, the synagogue leader, Dr. Eric Kaplan, told me his story.

Dr. Kaplan and his wife were a handsome couple in their fifties when they became caught up in America's obsession with looking younger. Though he had a medical background and should have investigated before acting, he followed the urging of friends and arranged for his wife and himself to be injected with Botox to erase a few barely perceptible wrinkles on their faces. Unfortunately, the doctor they went to injected them with black-market botulinum toxin that had not been diluted to one-twentieth of its potency, as should have been done. Two days later, they were both rushed to the emergency room, totally paralyzed, and put on life support. For six months, they hovered between life and death, unable to speak, move a finger, or open their eyes. Doctors were baffled as to how to treat them; no one had ever survived poisoning by that strong a dose of botulism. Ultimately, thanks to devoted medical care, their indomitable will, and the love of family and friends, they came out of their paralysis. By the time I met them, the Kaplans were almost fully recovered, with only a few lingering limitations.

In a book he wrote about his ordeal, entitled *Dying to Be Young*, Dr. Kaplan writes, "People have asked me over and over why I had Botox injections. While I was lying in the hospital incapable of moving a single muscle, I asked myself that question many times. The answer is simple: vanity. We live in a world obsessed with how we look." He castigates himself for being so fearful of looking his age and for taking seriously a remark that the comedian Billy Crystal meant as a joke: "It is better to look good than to feel good."

I am not opposed to cosmetic surgery if it will correct physical anomalies and help people feel better about themselves, but I worry about people's unrealistic expectations as to what will change. Are they setting themselves up for disappointment?

I remember seeing a cosmetic surgeon in a television interview as he described how he gets to know a prospective patient. She tells him what she would like changed. He assures her he can do that, then he holds a mirror up to her face and says, "See, you look better already." If she doesn't laugh, he worries that he may not be able to help her. The problem of self-loathing might go too deep for a few cosmetic changes to correct.

But we tend to prefer the quick fix, the easy technological solution, over the hard work that may be the only way of genuinely dealing with our issues. Years ago, when I was trying to improve my tennis game, I went into a sporting goods store to inquire about a new titanium racket that I had seen advertised. The clerk told me, "Don't waste your money. Spend it on lessons. A bad player with an expensive racket is still a bad player." In much the same way, a person with a poor self-image might be better advised to work on her self-image problem with a therapist rather than tinker with her external appearance. Otherwise, she may end up as a woman with a straighter nose but the same poor self-image.

To be told that beauty shines from within, from the core of a person who is in love with life and awake to its joys, may seem like a pious attempt to mollify someone who has not been blessed with external good looks, but it happens to be true. You may attract a few more interested stares, but you will never really be beautiful until, at your core, you like yourself. Dr. Kaplan also writes: "You can fool others with your outward appearance but you know what is inside. . . . [Or is] that the very thing that people are trying to avoid, looking inside for self-worth and contentment? . . . How do we get out of the competitive rat race that compels us to look outside ourselves for approval and self-worth? It all begins with gratitude and self-awareness, being thankful for who you are and what you have."

The fact remains that being good-looking is an advantage in life, often an unfair advantage. What can you do if you haven't been blessed with good looks and you feel that will keep you from getting what you crave in life? You can realize that good looks are certainly helpful but are not the only gift a person can be blessed with. If you were lucky enough to have been born healthy to wise and responsible parents, that in the long run may serve you better than good looks. If you are athletically gifted, you will be the envy of your teenage peers as you and they pass through adolescence, and that may endow you with a lifetime's worth of confidence. Intelligence, a high energy level, and a sense of humor are gifts that will serve you well at any age and will not fade as early as the blessing of physical appearance will. Stunningly beautiful women, like very wealthy women, can never be sure why people are showing interest in them. One of the most beautiful women I know once told me that she was never able to be a carefree teenager; grown men were asking her out when she was fifteen.

And if you are one of the ones lucky enough to inherit strikingly good looks, the first thing I would say to you is: Don't panic at the prospect of losing part of yourself, a cherished part of yourself, as you grow older. There will be plenty of the real you left. If you have invested a large part of your identity in your appearance, if you have defined yourself in your own mind and if others have defined you first and foremost by your good looks, it can be a deeply upsetting thing to see that start to slip away. You may find yourself worrying if you will be the same person you have been until now if one of the most conspicuous things about you is no longer what it has been. But it may be that you will have no choice except to reinvent yourself, building on the confidence you developed when you could count on your attractiveness to get people to give you the benefit of the doubt.

Often there is a glow to people who were beautiful when they were young that remains with them as they age, but now it comes not from their outward appearance but from their having learned to like themselves, not from artificially hiding the truth about their looks. There is a strange incident in chapter 12 of the book of Genesis. During one of the periodic famines that afflicted the land of Canaan, Abraham and his wife, Sarah, take their flocks and herds and migrate to Egypt, where there is always pasture. As they are about to cross the border into Egypt, Abraham says to his wife, "I know what a beautiful woman you are. If the Egyptians see you and think, She is his wife, they may kill me and let you live. Please say that you are my sister that I may remain alive thanks to you" (Genesis 12:10–13). That is precisely what happens. Pharaoh is smitten by Sarah's beauty and takes her into his harem, and God has to intervene to preserve her chastity. I have often taught that story as an example of good people doing bad things if they fear for their lives. But there is another problem with that tale beyond Abraham's shamefully selfish behavior. According to the biblical chronology, Abraham was in his eighties when that incident took place, and Sarah was only a few years younger. How beautiful could a seventy-five-year-old woman be to drive men wild with lust?

One commentator has suggested an answer that I like. It is understandable that Abraham should have thought that Sarah was beautiful. He probably remembered her as a young bride. He remembered all that they had shared together. In his eyes, she was still beautiful. But that only explains Abraham. Why did Pharaoh find her beautiful? The commentator's answer: Sarah was still beautiful because she lived with someone who saw her as beautiful and kept telling her so, which gave her a sense of confidence and well-being that radiated outward.

My advice to the woman who is afraid that age will wither her beauty would be to make sure that there are people in your life who knew you at your loveliest and still see you that way. Beyond that, be grateful for the benefits that looking good confers, but be aware that like so many things in life, it is a gift that does not last forever. Instead of striving to deny the changes that the years bring, use those years to prepare yourself for the person you will be when you can no longer define yourself primarily by your appearance. Author Sara Davidson writes about undergoing minor cosmetic surgery, only to have her teenage daughter burst into tears and tell her, "I want a mother who has wrinkles and is wise, not someone trying to look young with a plastic face." A Colorado woman wrote in to a local newspaper, "As someone who has lost several women friends to early death, I never regret growing older and finding another gray hair, for many never have that privilege."

If you have come to terms with the fact that you may not look as attractive as you once did when you grow older, how do you handle that other dimension of intimidating loss associated with the passage of years, the prospect that your body, and maybe even your mind, will no longer be able to do things that it once could do? Can you accept having to replace your weekly game of tennis singles with playing doubles, which you once scorned as "chess in sneakers"? Will you be offended if you offer to join your teenage son's touch football game, and he suggests that you referee instead?

I have a friend who is one of America's leading gerontologists, an authority on the aging process. For several years, we vacationed together in Arizona and would begin our day with a three-mile walk and some thoughtful conversation. One day, I mentioned to him that I would be turning seventy in a few weeks and that I found the prospect daunting. I told him that turning fifty had not bothered me at all. After all, I come out of a tradition that values wisdom and experience over the physical vigor of youth. Turning sixty had not bothered me either. But seventy, I confessed, felt old. He said to me, "Harold, you're operating with an out-of-date mind-set. A generation ago, when you were growing up, seventy probably *was* old. I would bet that if your father was living at seventy, he was an old man already. Social Security, created at about the time that you were born, assumed that few people would live very long beyond retirement at sixty-five. But things are different now. I bet your father at seventy could not have started his day with a three-mile walk at a fifteen-minute-per-mile pace or put in a half hour on the treadmill before dinner the way you do. To be seventy today is more like being fifty when you were growing up."

I found his words comforting and have often recalled them in the years since that morning. Most days I even believe them. (My friend is in his eighties and still creative and vigorous.) But then there are days when I have my doubts. I bend down to pick something up and experience a touch of lightheadedness when I stand up straight again. I go downstairs to get something out of the freezer, and by the time I get to the freezer, I've forgotten what it was I had gone there for. Then climbing back upstairs leaves me winded.

When I was a young rabbi, I often suspected that the secret of my success was not my knowledge of Scripture or my eloquent preaching but my ability to remember names. I could meet people once and recognize them by name a week or two later. It made them feel valued, taken seriously by their rabbi. Today I need to be reminded of the names of people I've known for years.

There are days when I am inclined to agree with Nora Ephron, who turned her lament about growing older into the number one best seller *I Feel Bad About My Neck*. She writes, "I try as much as possible not to look in the mirror. If I pass a mirror, I avert my eyes. If I must look into it, I begin by squinting, so that if anything really bad is looking back at me, I am already halfway to closing my eyes to ward off the sight. . . . Every so often, I read a book about aging and whoever's writing it says it's great to be old. It's great to be wise and sage and mellow; it's great to be at the point where you understand just what matters in life. I can't stand people who say things like this."

We cannot defer the physical decline that comes with age indefinitely, but there are things we can do to stay young longer and postpone the inevitable. I endorse the philosophy of Mel Zuckerman, founder of the fitness resort Canyon Ranch, who likes to say, "My goal is to die young—as late as possible." The biblical injunction to deal compassionately with the elderly (Leviticus 19:32) has been interpreted to mean, Be kind to the old person you will one day become. Don't burden that old man or woman with the consequences of the bad habits of your younger years. The physically gifted baseball star Mickey Mantle, whose father and uncle died young, assumed that he would die young as well, and, as a result, he lived a wild and carefree life. Shortly before his death at age sixty-three, he lamented, "If I'd known I was going to live this long, I'd have taken better care of myself." Recent medical research is indicating how much of a difference even moderate exercise can make in a person's weight, mood, and memory. An article in *The New York Times* states, "In humans, exercise improves what scientists call 'executive function,' the set of abilities that allows you to select behavior that's appropriate to the situation, inhibit inappropriate behavior and focus on the job at hand. . . . When inactive people get more exercise, even starting in their 70s, their executive function improves. . . . Exercise is also strongly associated with a reduced risk of dementia late in life." I read that and I thought of my parents' generation, for whom a vacation meant sitting on the porch of a hotel and being fed three generous meals a day. I have to believe that contributed to their getting old sooner.

Then there are those people who worry about growing older for fear they will turn into someone different from the person they have been, someone they do not want to be. One person said to me, "I don't mind growing to look like my father. I just don't want to *become* my father. My father, when he turned sixty, did some irresponsible things that hurt the family in an effort to feel young again, and I would never want to do that to my family." Another told me, "My mother, in her later years, became someone she had never been before, cranky and needy and hypercritical of everyone around her, to the point where my children didn't want to visit her anymore. I don't want to end up like that."

I would tell those people, You are not your father or mother. You're a different person, and the fact that you can see the wrongness of what your parent did proves that you're a different person. Granted, your parents were your primary role models when you were growing up, but that doesn't mean you have to follow their every example. If you make the effort, you can break the pattern, and the fact that you feel so strongly about the example your parents set should give you the energy and the determination to do that. As I am constantly telling people, "You don't have to be a prisoner of your past. You can be the architect of your future." Maybe you can't control biology and genetics when it comes to resembling your parents, but you can control behavior.

The loss of our looks or our athletic ability may dismay us, but for many of us, the most terrifying aspect of growing old is the increased risk of serious, debilitating illness. We worry that we will lose the ability to do the things that we enjoy as well as the things that define us—our work, our volunteer activities, our most intimate moments with our loved ones. Dr. Thomas Graboys, a prominent Boston physician, describes his struggle with Parkinson's disease in an affecting memoir, *Life in the Balance*. Despite his medical expertise, Dr. Graboys denied the early symptoms of his illness, although he would easily have recognized them in a patient and although colleagues around him saw it. He refused to accept the likelihood that he would soon have to give up the activities that gave his life meaning. He writes, "Life without my work would be no life at all. . . . Being a physician was everything to me. It was the reason I got up in the morning. It was an integral part of my identity and my sense of self-worth. It was the symbol of everything I had once been, decisive, quick-thinking, analytical and in control, but could no longer be." The day he had to tell his colleagues and patients that he could no longer continue to practice as a doctor, an announcement they heard with sorrow but also a measure of relief because they had seen him deteriorate, was a profoundly sad moment. The old Thomas Graboys was no longer there and was being mourned.

Along with the shattering sense of loss that accompanied his giving up the professional life he had worked so hard to excel at, Graboys worried about the burden his illness would place on his wife, and even worried about whether she would remain with him. It was a second marriage, only a few years in duration; his first wife had died of cancer some years earlier, and he remembered how painful it was for him to see her slip away. This was not the life he had promised his new bride when she agreed to marry a handsome, virile, successful physician. He mused, "What if you fell in love and the person told you he was terminally ill? Would you still marry him? What if you married and then learned that your [mate] had a life-threatening illness? Would you stay with him?"

In his case, his wife has stayed with him, without reservation and without expressing self-pity. But that isn't always what happens. When my book *When Bad Things Happen to Good People* came out, I got thousands of letters from people who shared their stories with me. Among them were several dozen letters from women telling me that when they became seriously ill or learned they had a seriously ill child, their husbands left them. One wrote, "I can't understand it. I really thought he loved me and he loved the children." I got very few letters from men telling me that their wives left them when they grew ill. I don't think it is simply a matter of women being more compassionate and family oriented. I suspect that many of the men who left their families did in fact love them and felt bad for them. But often, when a man realizes how little he can do to make a case of multiple sclerosis or breast cancer go away, his sense of helplessness, of being unable to do anything for a person he loves, is so overwhelming that all he can do is run away from it. Had such a husband shared his anguish with me, I could have told him how helpful it would have been for him just to remain at his wife's (or child's) side, holding her hand and easing her fear of abandonment.

Dr. Graboys goes on to write, "I struggle not to let the disease define me, but to live as fully as I can within the limitations imposed by the disease." And that is all any of us can do. We can concentrate on continuing to do the things we are still capable of, with the parts of our bodies that still work. We can join a support group of people dealing with the same ailment, sharing coping strategies and seeing examples of people going through what we are going through and making the most of it. We can gain strength by being able to help them in a way that few outsiders can. We can challenge our friends, our church and synagogue communities to prove their willingness to live their faith by helping us where we most need help. I have known congregations that organized volunteers to drive ill people to and from doctors' appointments or shovel the snow off their driveways.

If we can no longer be the people we used to be, we can reinvent ourselves not as victims of misfortune, as people to be pitied, but as men and women who inspire others with our fortitude, people who can put a face on the need for research to cure a given condition or illness, as Christopher Reeve did with spinal cord injury, as Michael J. Fox did for Parkinson's disease, as friends of mine who are not famous did to raise money for research into progeria.

I have seen such transformations in people I have known. I especially remember one woman who always struck me as being terribly self-involved until she was diagnosed with cancer, and then, to everyone's amazement, a side of her that no one had ever seen emerged. She became the one who would brighten the radiation therapy waiting room with jokes and compliments.

My experience with the desperately ill has taught me that they are not so afraid of dying. What frightens them most is the fear of being abandoned while they are still alive, abandoned by people who care about them but who see in the seriously ill a foretaste of what might be in store for themselves and cannot handle it or by people who want to help but feel inadequate. We can do a great deal to calm the fears of the seriously ill simply by being there for them, sitting quietly with them and assuring them that we will not abandon them.

No discussion of the physical and emotional perils of growing old would be complete without confronting what is for many people the most terrifying prospect of all, the loss of self, the fear that our minds will deteriorate to the point where we will no longer know who we are. Illness is always a concern for people as they grow older. When I was younger, the illness that frightened people most was cancer. Heart attacks were less dreadful because they were sudden, over in a moment. But when it came to cancer, people could not even bring themselves to utter the word, as if saying it out loud would make it happen. They would use readily understood code words or invent euphemisms. Today, fear of cancer takes second place to the fear of Alzheimer's disease. Typically, I heard one woman say, "If I get cancer, I can fight it. They are coming up with new things all the time. I can work with my doctor to buy more time, to keep me comfortable. But with Alzheimer's, there is no me there anymore to fight the battle."

Alice Munro's moving short story "The Bear Came Over the Mountain" (the movie version was titled *Away from Her*) portrays a husband's frustration as his wife gradually slips away from him and from their normal life. It started with little things. She would label the kitchen drawers, "Cutlery," "Dish Towels," "Knives," because she no longer trusted herself to remember what the items inside were called. Then one day she called him from town because she could no longer find her way home. He finally has to institutionalize her, and when he visits her there, she doesn't recognize him. He realizes that she and the other residents "were living a busy life inside their heads . . . a life that in most cases could not very well be described or alluded to in front of visitors."

That is what makes Alzheimer's disease unique in its power to frighten and frustrate. I have seen the terrifying power of Alzheimer's in its earliest stages, when its victims were still lucid enough to know what was happening to them. They were afraid not only for themselves and what they would be losing (essentially everything that made life meaningful for them); they were also terrified at the prospect of what they would be imposing on their loved ones and how powerless those loved ones would be to help them cope. Other serious illnesses afflict the patient and leave to the doctors and loved ones the challenge of easing the pain and reassuring the patient that he or she is still loved and cared for. We can visit, we can hold hands and pray with the patient, and we can feel that we are doing something to help. But with Alzheimer's, it is we, the friends and family, who ache and grieve and feel powerless. When people have turned to me for advice on dealing with an Alzheimer's-afflicted spouse or parent, I have had only two things to recommend. First, keep on visiting them, caring about them, bringing them gifts and flowers, as a way of maintaining your own sense of loyalty and integrity ("She may not know who I am, but I know who I am"). Don't let your sense of inadequacy or your fear that you might be looking at "coming attractions" of your own fate keep you away. Second, just in case the patient is, even intermittently, aware of what is going on but incapable of expressing it, keep showing the love.

Why do we age? Why do our bodies begin to give out as the years accumulate? When our son was dying of progeria, a disease that accelerates the aging process and afflicts young children with the ailments of old age, I tried to learn everything I could about the natural course of aging. I learned that one theory among biologists is that all living creatures are programmed to reproduce, to perpetuate the species by passing on their DNA to the next generation, and then to disappear to make room for the next generation. Some insects live for barely a day, just long enough to deposit an egg somewhere that will hatch into another here-today-gone-tomorrow insect. Following that design, human beings are at their healthiest, most vigorous, and most attractive during their peak reproductive years. After that, according to this theory, Nature seems to say to us, Who needs you? After we have fulfilled the biblical injunction to "be fruitful and multiply," our gums recede and we need root canal work. Women's breasts sag and men's prostates swell. Our cells' ability to repair themselves diminishes, and we become vulnerable to all sorts of diseases. This theory suggests that Mother Nature is looking at us as if we were an old car and preparing to trade us in for a newer model.

I refuse to accept that perspective. The glory of the human race is that we have learned to do so many things to compensate for what Nature fails to do for us. We wear clothing to protect our bodies. We build houses, heating them in winter and cooling them in summer. We have invented eyeglasses, hearing aids, prosthetic limbs. We have developed vaccines to prevent illnesses and antibiotics to cure them. We have learned to transplant organs and bone marrow. To Nature's challenge, Who needs you?, we defiantly proclaim, We're still here.

In the Bible, we often read of angels appearing to people at crucial moments of their lives to bring them a word from God. We don't have to picture them as ethereal creatures with wings and halos; they usually seem to take on human form. But one interesting thing about angels sent by God is that when they have completed their mission, they disappear, which happens to the angel who tells Samson's mother that she will have a special child in Judges 13, and to the angels who come to Abraham and to Lot in Genesis 19. One by one, their message delivered, they vanish.

That is the difference between angels and human beings, and between human beings and less advanced forms of life. We find ample reason to go on living even when our biological mission has been completed. Nature may have designed us to bear and raise our young and then fade away, but as we saw in our discussion of earthquakes and hurricanes, Nature can be morally shallow. Nature makes the rules for things like sex and childbirth, health and illness. But Nature cannot comprehend such qualities as love, wisdom, or creativity. We cannot expect Nature to understand our drive to see grandchildren grow up, to read (or write) another book, to hear a symphony, follow a pennant race, or take pleasure in the emergence of a talented young actor or actress. That is why we, in the last third of our lives, fight back against the natural process of decay. It is not out of greed or vanity. It is because there are things we still want to do and enjoy, proudly and defiantly proclaiming that we are not yet finished living.

This brings us to one more aspect of the fear too often associated with growing older, the fear that society no longer has use for us. Old people get in the way. They walk slowly; they drive slowly. They are forgetful. They complain endlessly about their ailments. They are stooped and wrinkled, and worst of all, they convey to us the unwelcome message, One day this will be you. If Kipling's "cruel looking-glass" conveys a dismaying image to a forty-five-year-old woman, imagine what it says to a man or woman a few decades older.

Sara Davidson emerged as one of the voices of the Boomer (formerly Baby Boom) generation with her book *Loose Change.* Then, when she turned fifty, she captured the angst of her contemporaries in another book, *LEAP!* Early in the book, she defines her overriding concern: "What am I supposed to do for the next thirty years? I've raised my children, written bestsellers, had deep love. . . . Why am I still here?" She goes on, "There's a new life stage—after fifty and before eighty—and we're the ones whose mission it will be to figure out what to do with it."

Davidson may have an ally in her struggle that she is not aware of. It is to be found in the vast number of people who share her concerns: I will be living longer; how do I get society to take me seriously and not dismiss me to a life of shuffleboard and medical appointments? Her salvation may be found in three words: Baby Boom generation. There is reason to anticipate that businesses and governmental agencies will take the concerns of Sara Davidson and her contemporaries more seriously than it has taken those of the aging population until now, not only because people are living longer but because there are so many of them.

The generation of people born between 1946 and 1964, children born to veterans returning from the military in an age of prosperity and economic expansion, has been regularly described by demographers as "the pig in the python," a massive bulge in the population statistics, overwhelmingly outnumbering those born in the decades of the Depression and World War II and those born in the mid-1960s and 1970s, when many young adults deferred marriage and parenthood. Their sheer numbers doomed them to overcrowded schools (I remember double shifts in junior high and high school, with some pupils scheduled for lunch at 10:30 in the morning) and fierce competition for admission to the better colleges. But in a political and economic democracy, numbers count. If you are in the business of selling something, you would like it to be something that a lot of people will want to buy. You will "go hunting where the ducks are," and in this case, the "ducks" were the millions of young people known as Baby Boomers. Their numbers compelled society to run after them, ask them what they wanted, and see to it that their wants and needs were met. When Boomers were teenagers, Hollywood made movies and record companies produced music almost exclusively for and about teenagers. As the Baby Boom generation married and became parents, the bookstores and television schedules were geared to the questions and interests of young parents, and automobile makers rediscovered the station wagon. At every stage of life, they found society asking them what they wanted and offering to sell it to them. And now that the first wave of Boomers are in their sixties, I can imagine that society will finally get around to taking the problems of mature aging adults very seriously. To cite one example, the issue of universal health care has been on the political agenda since Harry Truman was president. Only now, as the Boomer generation begins to worry about the illnesses that accompany advancing years, is the topic finally gaining some traction. Of all the things that frighten us when we look into the future, this may be the only one where we can look to society to make things easier. There will be just too many aging adults for America to ignore them. Boomers will be living longer, maybe as much as thirty years longer than their parents did if obesity or epidemics don't intervene, and they will continue to reshape society as they have done in every decade since they were children.

But not everything that concerns us about growing old can be solved by governmental action or by economic interests trying to sell us things. Our values as a society have to change as well. There will be generations of people after the Boomers, and they too will grow old in time. Robert Sapolsky has written in *Monkeyluv,* "Geriatric depression is epidemic in our society and virtually non-existent in others. Why? Different environments [prevail] in different societies, in which old age can mean being a powerful village elder or an infantilized has-been put out to a shuffleboard pasture." Daniel Goleman, author of the important books *Emotional Intelligence* and *Social Intelligence,* describes how his widowed mother, when she retired from teaching at the local college, made a room in her home available free of charge to a graduate student who would provide her with some human companionship. She gave priority to students from Asia, where the culture esteems the elderly more than most Americans do.

How can we get our culture to take on that perspective, cherishing wisdom and experience more than smooth skin and youthful vigor? It won't be easy, given that things are changing so rapidly in our world that experience isn't as valuable as it used to be. I would like to think that we could take a step in that direction by coming to understand and to teach our children that some truths are eternal and don't change as technology changes. But perhaps the most effective argument for treating the elderly with dignity is the simplest: Make old age a desirable destination because that is where we are all headed. If the appeal to altruism and generosity doesn't work, try self-interest.

Everyone is familiar with the fifth of the Ten Commandments, "Honor your father and your mother." But have you ever carefully read the full text of that verse? "Honor your father and your mother *that your days may be long* on the land that the Lord your God gives you" (Exodus 20:12; my emphasis). Treating elderly parents with respect may help *them* live longer, but how does it do the same for you? Maybe the import of the commandment is: If you treat your aged parents well even when you no longer need them to take care of you (and the commandments were addressed to mature adults, not to children), then you will be voting for a society in which all the elderly are treated with respect and consulted for their wisdom. When that happens, you will be able to look forward to a long and happy life, not in the sense that you will necessarily live longer but in the sense that you will have no reason to dread growing old for fear that people will dismiss you as irrelevant.

The survival of so many currently young people into their eighties and nineties will likely force society to see old age differently. No longer merely individuals who have not died yet, they will represent a new stage in life.

In the beginning, there were only two stages of life, adults and children, or in the view of some scholars, adults and small adults. For many generations, children dressed like grown-ups and were expected to work to the limits of their ability. Then, over time, we "invented" adolescence. We recognized that young people in their teens, who had previously been treated virtually as adults and sent out to work as soon as they were able, were no longer children but lacked the maturity and education to function fully as adults. We extended the years of their education and postponed their entry into marriage and the workforce. Adolescents soon developed their own culture, their own language, their own modes of dress. In the last century, we recognized young adulthood as a separate stage: people beyond the teen years, ready to assume some adult responsibilities—driving, drinking, voting, earning money—but still in graduate school or apprenticeship positions, usually not ready to take on the responsibilities of marriage and family. We reluctantly recognized that we could not expect them, as we might expect teenagers, to delay sexual experience, and we reluctantly came to accept the readiness of two young adults to live together in a relationship that carried no necessary assumption of permanence. Once again, they had their own culture, dress, favorite television programs, and nightclubs at which older and younger people were not welcome.

The twenty-first century seems poised to recognize the emergence of another new life stage, the young-old, senior but not senile. The needs and interests of men and women in their seventies are as different from those of people in their fifties as the world of a sixteen-year-old is from the world of an eleven-year-old. As one comedian put it, you know you're there when the phone numbers in your little black book are no longer girl-friends but doctors. Based on my friendship with many young-old people, though, I've come to learn that whatever else may be in those little black books, many of them contain appointments at the various schools and centers where they volunteer to put their free time to good use. Their concerns are typically health, adequate financial resources, having a sense of meaning in their lives without employment, and being taken seriously by society. (When my father-in-law was in his eighties and went to a new young doctor to ask about a problem that would ultimately cause his death a few years later, the doctor told him, "Let's not do anything about it. How much longer do you expect to live anyway?")

I believe it is time to call a halt to the war between the generations, between the people Philip Roth in a recent novel called the "not-yets" and the "no-longers," which like most conflicts is fueled by fear and resentment. Older people resent younger ones for their noise, their vitality, the possibilities that are still available to them, and a host of other reasons. We have seen the emergence of adult-only communities where no one younger than fifty-five is welcome to settle, and visiting grandchildren are barely tolerated.

The one religious obligation I have worked hardest to meet in my personal and professional life has been the commandment to see every human being as fashioned in the image of God: the attractive and the plain, the pleasant and the contentious, the physically perfect and the physically or developmentally disabled, the articulate and the stammerers. All of them are manifestations of a God who is big enough to encompass them all. And it hasn't always been easy. Old people too often have trouble discerning the image of God in the boisterous young. I wish they could learn to see the liveliness and the emerging sexuality of the young as manifestations of God. Can we really not remember what we were like at that age? Rather than letting their encounters with the young remind them of what they have lost or left behind, I wish they would let the young people they know brighten their world with their liveliness. Let our encounters with the young provoke fond memories rather than resentment and envy, memories of a time when we were young; we might even add a silent prayer of gratitude that those years of sexual and professional uncertainty are well behind us. I have known geriatric hospital and hospice patients who found themselves capable of flirting with an attractive young nurse or a good-looking attendant. I have known many men and women in their eighties who retained, and even sharpened, their sense of humor in conversations with their grandchildren. And I have to believe that they enjoyed their lives more than did the senior citizens who looked at the young with unconcealed resentment.

I also wish that young and middle-aged men and women would stop regarding the elderly as a "cruel looking-glass" reflecting back at them their worst fears of how they will end up and instead come to see them as bearers of God's image. Let them see the length of days as an instance of God's grace, a gift that may be awaiting them as well. Let them say to themselves, If God has been around for millions of years, then the older one gets, the more one comes to resemble God. Let them learn to see the elderly at the very least as survivors, no small achievement, and perhaps even to see them as sources of wisdom, men and women who can use their recollections of decades past not to lament the passing of the "good old days," but to put the social and political events of today into a deeper perspective. Sara Davidson notes that " 'masters' has become the [politically correct] word for 'older' in athletic competitions," and she responds favorably to the usage, saying, "I like the concept of mastery." Many old people have seen remarkable things; many have done remarkable things; many have learned important lessons in the course of their lives, and we would do well to learn from them. Doctor friends have shared with me stories of taking the time to chat with elderly patients whom they might have been tempted to write off as terminal cases waiting to die, and discovering so much of interest and value about them. After all, they had not always been sick old men and women. One had been an actress on Broadway, one had been chief of staff to a prominent senator, another had helped to liberate one of the concentration camps at the end of World War II, and still another was a former Olympic fencer. They were fascinating people, once we learned to see beyond the surface of "old, sick, and close to death."

Unless we are planning on dying young, we do ourselves and others a disservice when we make old age something to be feared. Life is not a resource to be used up, so that the older we get, the less life we have left. Life is the accumulation of wisdom, love, and experience, of people encountered and obstacles overcome. The longer we live, the more life we will possess. Rather than fear the bad news in the mirror, let us claim as our own the words of the late actor Ossie Davis: "Age is that point of elevation from which it is easier to see who you are. . . . Age makes knowledge, tempers knowledge with experience, and out of that comes the possibility of wisdom." Or in words attributed to George Bernard Shaw, "Life is no brief candle for me. It is . . . a splendid torch . . . and I want to make it burn as brightly as possible before handing it on to future generations."

8

*

The World Is a Narrow Bridge

THE FEAR OF DEATH

> A free man thinks of death least of all things, and his
> wisdom is a meditation of life, not of death.
>
> SPINOZA, *Ethics*

> Rather than live on in the hearts and minds of my fellow
> men, I'd prefer to live on in my apartment.
>
> WOODY ALLEN

When I was fifteen years old, I fell in love with the biblical book of Ecclesiastes. I loved Ecclesiastes then for
much the same reasons that my fifteen-year-old grandson loves
Jon Stewart and *The Daily Show* on television, for the same
reasons that fifteen-year-olds have for decades responded to
J. D. Salinger's novel *The Catcher in the Rye*—because it
seemed to challenge the hypocritical pieties of the adult world
that controlled my life. "All is vanity. What does a man gain
from all the toil at which he toils under the sun?" (Ecclesiastes 1:2). "I amassed silver and gold, more than anyone before
me . . . and it was all futile, there was no real value to it"
(2:8–11). "Be not excessively righteous nor excessively wise
lest you bring yourself to destruction" (7:16).

When I was thirty-five years old and working toward a doctoral degree in the Bible, I returned to the study of Ecclesiastes and discovered another dimension of the anonymous sage who wrote it. Now I came to see him as a middle-aged man who worried that all he had worked so hard for—wealth, fame, pleasure—would ultimately disappear, and nothing would remain. He was asking, "What is worth investing my time and energy in? What will endure?"

Then, the year I turned fifty, my father died, and I became the oldest living member of my family. I turned again to Ecclesiastes, making it the focus of my book *When All You've Ever Wanted Isn't Enough*, and for the third time in my life, I thought I finally understood it. Now I saw the author of Ecclesiastes as an old man, terrified at the prospect of dying. Now what frightened him was not the thought that everything he had worked for would disappear. It was the fear that *he* would disappear. The prospect of dying cast a pall over everything he had done and everything he still yearned to do, shrouding it with an air of futility. He had met every challenge life had put to him, but he would not be able to meet the challenge of defeating death. Ernest Becker, in his classic work *The Denial of Death*, writes, "Of all things that move men, one of the principal ones is the terror of death. . . . It is the basic fear that influences all others, a fear from which no one is immune."

All living things, when faced with danger, struggle to escape and survive. But only human beings are haunted by the knowledge of their ultimate mortality even when they are not in mortal danger. Some years ago, I heard a lecture on the biblical story of Adam and Eve in the Garden of Eden. The speaker asked, "What was the knowledge that Adam and Eve acquired when they ate the fruit of the Tree of Knowledge of Good and

Bad? Was the story meant to teach us that they learned that some things are good and others are bad, that they acquired a conscience? Or was the story less about the meaning of the fruit and more about their act of disobedience, that having been given one rule, they broke it?"

The speaker said that by eating the fruit, they learned something that was both good and bad. They learned that one day they would die, and having learned how brief and fragile a human life could be, they would never again be able to think of their lives in the same way. God's warning to the first humans, "for on the day you eat of it, you will die" (Genesis 2:17), would be understood to mean not that they would die instantly (they didn't) but that they would realize, in a way no other creature does, that they were fated one day to die.

The question of how the knowledge of our inevitable death can be called both "good and bad" is an important one that we will have to deal with. But the speaker went on to justify his interpretation by calling our attention to what happens immediately after Adam and Eve eat the forbidden fruit. The very next verse tells us they realized that they were naked and they were embarrassed (Genesis 3:7). Why were they embarrassed, given that there was literally no one else in the world to see them in their nakedness? They were embarrassed to have bodies, not because there was anything wrong with their bodies, some parts too big and others too small, but because it was their bodies that made them mortal, vulnerable to illness, injury, and death. Their bodies would one day betray them, made up as they were of bones that could break, organs that could fail, blood that could become infected. If it weren't for their physical bodies, they would be able to go on living eternally.

We human beings are caught up in a perpetual struggle between the yearnings of the spirit and the demands of the body. No matter how much we cultivate the spirit, no matter how much we strive to subordinate our bodies to it through prayer, dieting, and sexual restraint, we can never escape the realization that in the end, our physical bodies will have the ultimate victory. They will give out, and, no matter how pious we are, we will die.

The fact that only the human being is burdened every day of his life by the knowledge of death's inevitability may explain why the author of the Twenty-third Psalm speaks of the "valley of the *shadow* of death." Long before someone comes to the point of actually dying, the prospect of death, the inevitability of death, casts a shadow over his days.

The knowledge of our mortality spurs people to do great things in an effort to cheat death. Families have children so that their name, their values, and their DNA will live on into the next generation. People who never have children find other ways of achieving a form of immortality. Artists, writers, and composers labor to fashion works of art that future generations will continue to cherish. Doctors strive to find cures for diseases, whether in the hope that future generations will invoke their names with gratitude, the way we speak of the Salk vaccine against polio, or as a symbolic victory for the human spirit in the fight against disease. Physician and author Dr. Sherwin Nuland has written, "Of all the professions, medicine is one most likely to attract people with high personal anxieties about dying. We become doctors because our ability to cure gives us power over the death of which we are so afraid."

If we were pure spirit, if we were angels, we could happily exist forever without worrying about illness, physical decline, and death. If we were only animals, we could live, age, and perish without the distraction of dreading the end of our lives. If we were pure spirit, we would never be seduced by gluttony, envy, or sexual desire. If we were bodies without souls, without conscience, we could indulge in our fill of sensual pleasure without pangs of guilt. But because we are unique creatures that combine body and spirit, we crave religion to guide and elevate us, and at the same time, we resent it for making us feel guilty whenever we are tempted to do things that most normal people are tempted to do. (I have long suspected that many anti-Semites are really feeling hatred for the Jew from Nazareth for imposing Christian morality on them.)

When we are young, we act on the assumption that our time is unlimited. Young people are not uncomfortable wasting time because they believe they have an endless supply of it. To them, middle age is unimaginably far off and death is too far over the horizon even to be glimpsed. It has been said that eighteen-year-old young men make the best soldiers and the worst drivers because they can't imagine they won't live forever. When I have had to officiate at the funeral of a young person, a victim of disease or accident, I have found adults to be saddened by the tragedy. But the dead young person's friends feel more angry than sad. They feel betrayed. "This is so unfair; this is not supposed to happen, " they say.

But soon enough, the time comes when those who survive have to come to terms with their mortality, when they realize that no matter how wisely they eat or how strenuously they exercise, they will not live forever. How then do they avoid the fate of Ecclesiastes, deciding that nothing matters because, despite their best efforts, they will die one day and the world will keep going without them?

It is when people confront these kinds of questions that they turn to religion. How does religion guide us in not letting the prospect of death cast a cloud of futility over our lives? Religious guidance typically goes in one of three directions. Sometimes religion tries to justify an individual's death as appropriate, part of God's plan. I have seen life and death in this world compared to a tapestry seen from the wrong side, a jumble of long and short threads fitting no discernible pattern. But seen from above, from God's perspective, the long threads, the knotted threads, and the threads cut short all fit together to make up a work of beauty. Or premature death may be a reward for having successfully completed one's life mission. Buddhism speaks of a death as "the drop of water returning to its source in the ocean." Or it may be seen as part of God's long-range plan, impossible for us on earth to comprehend.

Sometimes religion tries to banish the terror of death by assuring us that death is not real. It offers us a promise of the hereafter, a life beyond this life, a realm where our spirits will have shed their earthly bodies and will live on eternally. In heaven, we will still have a sense of who we are. We will recognize our loved ones. But everything that was wrong in this world, everything that was broken or imperfect, will be healed. In heaven, there will be no illness, no hunger, and no jealousy.

And sometimes religion promises us that, despite the limitations of our corporeal nature, we are capable of lives of such heroism and spiritual excellence that we will represent the triumph of the spirit over the flesh here on earth.

In his novel *The Bridge of San Luis Rey*, Thornton Wilder offers his solution to the question of why death often seems to interrupt an unfinished life. The book begins with an accident that claims the lives of five apparently unrelated people. A rope bridge over a chasm in a small Peruvian village gives way, sending the five people who were crossing it to their deaths. A young Catholic priest witnesses the accident, and it challenges his faith in the goodness of a world under God's direction. He sets out to investigate the lives of the five victims to see if in any way it was morally appropriate for them to die at that moment and in that manner. He discovers that in each case, the person's ability to enjoy life had been blocked by an excessive focus on the self and an inability to love. But each of them had recently resolved that problem and opened himself or herself to love. The priest's conclusion is that how long a person lives may be the least important measure of that person's life. Our lives are measured in breadth and depth, not only in length. The purpose of life is to learn to love, to learn to reach out beyond the self. When we have learned to do that, we will have reached our goal and will be ready to "graduate" from this life to a higher level.

The Bridge of San Luis Rey is a beautiful book that has comforted many people over the years, but in the end, I find Wilder's solution unsatisfying. Why should people whom we love be taken away from us just when they have learned to love us in return? Are we wrong to grieve for them if their death represents their "graduating" to a higher form of life? Wouldn't this world be a better place if people who were capable of sharing love remained on earth to bless us with their love? Are we all destined to suffer the fate of Romeo and Juliet and all the other star-crossed lovers of medieval and modern literature, to die just when love seems within reach? And why would Wilder write a book to warn us against learning to love because it might prove fatal? We are left having to believe either that death (not death in general but the death of a specific person at a specific time, someone we knew and cared about) is tragic because it reduces the amount of goodness in the world, in which case we are baffled as to why God permits it, or that death in our world is one necessary stage of a larger plan on God's part.

It can be tempting to fasten on to the idea that death need not be tragic because a better life awaits us on the other side. I remember seeing a cartoon that showed a husband and wife who had died arriving in heaven, which is a world of sunlight and soft music and comfortable places to sit and relax. The husband turns to his wife and says, "Just think. If we hadn't quit smoking and eaten all that oat bran, this could have been ours ten years sooner."

The notion of a life beyond this one came relatively late to the Judeo-Christian tradition. Most of the Hebrew Bible never speaks of it. In fact, the book of Job, the story of a good man who suffers terribly, where one would expect the defenders of orthodox theology to comfort Job with visions of heavenly bliss and reward, never mentions it at all. To the contrary, all the speakers in the book seem to agree that "there is hope for a tree; if it is cut down, it will renew itself. . . . But mortals languish and die. Man expires and then where is he?" (Job 14:7, 10).

It is only in the book of Daniel, the last book in the Hebrew canon to be written, that we first find explicit references to the idea that those who die tragically and heroically will be restored to a better, longer life through God's intervention (Daniel 12:2–3).

Most scholars believe that the impetus for the emergence of this idea was the Maccabean revolt against the Greeks, the story behind the festival of Hanukkah some 160 years B.C.E. Many pious Jews died defending their faith against the efforts of the Greek emperor to wipe it out. Even as in our time, people might have been willing to accept the tragic death of individuals, telling themselves that we don't know all the details behind God's designs, until the Holocaust forced them to reconsider their beliefs, so the experience of seeing the most faithful and heroic people killed in battles defending God drove many Judeans, unwilling to conclude that life was unfair, to insist that that could not be the final event of those people's lives. Sometimes that insistence led to anticipating the resurrection of the dead to live out the stolen years of their lives on earth, a doctrine that, after bitter disputes, found its way into the Jewish prayer book. Sometimes it led to a belief in a person's soul spending eternity in heaven with God and other pious souls.

Some people believe in life in heaven after death because it is the only thing that makes the troubles and tragedies of this life bearable. In the absence of any proof that there is no heaven, they cling to the faith that there must be. If God is all-powerful and loving, He should be both willing and able to provide a happy ending to our all-too-brief and frustrating lives on earth. If God could create life out of nothing, why can't He restore a life that was already there?

Benjamin Franklin, shortly before his death, penned his own obituary: "The body of B. Franklin, printer, like the cover of an old book, its contents torn out. . . . But the work shall not be wholly lost, for it will, as he believed, appear once more in a new and more perfect edition, corrected and amended by the Author."

I would like to believe it. It would be a source of immeasurable bliss to think that when I die, I would be reunited with my son and make up for all those years of being together that I was denied when he died at age fourteen. But that joyful possibility is one of the things that makes me skeptical about the notion of an afterlife. I learned early that the world is not designed to make me happy. Books and movies can be manipulated by their creators to have happy endings; real life doesn't always work out that way. More than that, I am uncomfortable with a faith system that posits a definition of God and then decides "what God has to do" in order to live up to their definition. It sounds a bit like saying, If the facts conflict with my theology, I would rather ignore the facts than question my theology.

My colleague Professor Neil Gillman, in his excellent study *The Death of Death*, points out something I had never noticed before. The last line of the Passover Seder, when Jews celebrate God's redeeming of our ancestors from bondage in Egypt, describes God destroying the Angel of Death, as if anticipating a parallel between the Egyptian Exodus and a deliverance from the enslavement to mortality that limits us. We may no longer be slaves to Pharaoh, but our bodies are slaves to the Angel of Death, who will one day come to claim us. On Passover, we yearn to be freed from that limitation.

My family and I will continue to end our Seder meal with that image, but as we do so, I am chastened by Gillman's cautionary words: "The surest way to trivialize any eschatological doctrine is to understand it as literal truth, as a prediction of events that will take place as they are described in some eventual future." To me, the vision of God destroying Death offers not the promise of physically living again or of living forever but a poetic expression of confidence that there are some things about a person who links his or her life with God—deeds of kindness, medical breakthroughs, great works of art—that permit that person to outlive even his or her own death.

A reality check would remind us that our bodies decay and return to the earth, but so many of our after-death fantasies assume that we will still have bodies, probably because we can't imagine what it would feel like to exist without them. I have always been drawn to the vision of the afterlife offered by Maimonides, the great Jewish philosopher of the twelfth century. He posited that, after we die, the righteous are rewarded by having their disembodied souls spend eternity in the presence of God, and the wicked are punished by missing out on that reward. My only problem with that view is that it assumes a duality, an essential divide between body and soul, which is more of a Greek notion than a biblical one.

Let me then offer my own belief on the subject: We don't have to be afraid of dying because it is not really death that scares us. We are afraid of not having lived. In my nearly fifty years as a clergyman, I have been at the bedside of many, many dying people, young and old, religious and freethinkers, successful in life and less successful. They taught me the profound truth that terminally ill people are not afraid of death. When you are very sick, when little by little your body stops being able to do the things it has always been able to do, death may be the only cure for what ails you. There are three things that terrify the very ill person more than the prospect of dying.

They are afraid of pain, they are afraid that people will

abandon them while they are still alive, and they are afraid that they will die having wasted their lives, having never accomplished anything that will cause people to remember them when they are gone. For most people, the prospect of nullification, of having left no mark on the world, is more frightening than the prospect of not living forever. The real fear of dying, I am convinced, is the fear that we will leave this world with our tasks unfinished, and the best way, indeed the only way, to defeat death is to live fearlessly and purposefully.

When it comes to the fear of pain and of abandonment, the best thing that has happened in my lifetime has been the emergence of the hospice movement. I was recently invited to address a conference of hospice workers and volunteers, and I began by congratulating them on having changed the average American's definition of a good death. Had you asked the average person a few years ago for his notion of a good death, he probably would have said "to go to sleep and not wake up," echoing Woody Allen's words, "I don't mind dying; I just don't want to be there when it happens." Today, hospice has taught us to define a good death as one that sees us surrounded by family and loved ones, giving us the opportunity to say good-bye, to thank them for having cared for us and shared their lives with us, leaving no words unspoken that need to be spoken.

And hospice has persuaded doctors to let go, to forgo uncomfortable, invasive treatments that would only bring the patient a few more days or weeks of discomfort. Doctors no longer see assigning a patient to hospice as giving up or admitting defeat. As one doctor put it, when it comes to the terminally ill, medical care should usually involve more care and less medicine.

American society has been slower, however, to recognize the need of the terminally ill for human companionship. Perhaps because we feel so inadequate to do anything helpful ("I never know what to say"), perhaps because it involves looking in the mirror and seeing a preview of our own mortality, we visit the terminally ill less often, we phone them less often, and we spend less time with them. I remember a colleague of mine, an outstanding rabbi and pastor, who once confided to me, "I have a congregant whom I like a lot. He's about my age, a good friend, an occasional tennis partner. He's in the hospital with cancer and doesn't have much time left. I know I ought to visit him, but for some reason I never get around to it." I suggested, "Might it be because when you visit him, you see yourself one day in that situation and that's scary?" David Kessler, author of *The Needs of the Dying*, has written, "We may never feel more alone than when we ourselves are dying." Elsewhere, Kessler pictures the hospitalized terminally ill person saying, "You can talk to me, you can talk about me. Just don't talk without me, as if I weren't here. I'm not dead yet."

Recently, a close friend had to bury his ninety-seven-year-old aunt. He told me that when he visited her at the assisted-living facility where she spent her last years, the staff would comment on his frequent visits, telling him, "You have no idea how many people here go for weeks and months without a single visitor."

I know from my own experience in hospitals and nursing homes that it is not pleasant visiting the seriously ill. We feel there is so little we can do for them. When we do bring ourselves to do it, we should realize that our presence, our caring enough to come, does a lot for the dying person. It may not extend her life, but it reassures her that people know that she is still very much alive. Kessler offers a beautiful image of what we can do when a loved one is dying. He suggests that we escort them to the door of death the way we would accompany a friend leaving on a journey to his or her gate at the airport. (Given today's airport rules, we might think of accompanying them to the security transit point.)

But in case after case the dying have taught me that what frightened them more than pain or loneliness was the fear that they had wasted their lives, that they had used up their allotted time on earth keeping busy but never really having lived. Earlier, I cited the theory that the knowledge Adam and Eve acquired when they ate the fruit of the Tree of Knowledge of Good and Evil, the knowledge that elevated them above the level of animals, was the knowledge that they would one day die, and I asked how that awareness of mortality could be called good and bad, as the Bible describes the fruit. The answer may be that death is not good (except where it brings release from unbearable suffering), but the knowledge that we are destined to die can be good if it moves us to take our choices and preferences more seriously. If our time is limited, we realize that what we put off today, we may never get around to doing. It has been said that death, like birth, provides life with a temporal frame, a beginning and an end. Without them, there can be no middle. In the words of Dr. Elisabeth Kübler-Ross, who wrote so meaningfully on the subject, "It is the denial of death that is partially responsible for people living empty, purposeless lives; for when you live as if you'll live forever, it becomes too easy to postpone the things you know you must do."

Death does not negate the meaning of our lives. Death helps to define our lives. Remember, the word "define" means "to set boundaries." Death marks the end of life in the same way that a period marks the end of a sentence. It doesn't rob the sentence of meaning; it clarifies what the meaning of the sentence is. Your life is not meaningless just because it doesn't go on forever. It is precisely because our lives do not go on forever that our choices and values have significance.

But what if we understand that we are mortal yet get the frightening feeling that we may be running out of time with a large part of our agenda unfinished? What if, as we grow older and notice changes in our health and vigor, as we read more obituary notices for people our age and younger, we find ourselves thinking less about life and more about the prospect of dying? To speak of death in the abstract, to speak of the inevitability of death for all mankind, is a philosophical-theological conversation. To confront the prospect of one's own imminent death is an act of immense courage. My friend Forrest Church, a Unitarian minister in New York and author of a dozen books, recently sent me the manuscript of his next book. In an accompanying note, he told me that this book would be his last; he was dying of esophageal cancer. The book would be called *Love and Death*.

How does a man who has dealt with death professionally for years deal with the prospect of his own death? First, he overcomes the temptation to blame himself for contracting a fatal illness, not asking himself, "What did I do to deserve this?" whether in terms of unhealthy living or moral misbehavior. Too often, asking why either becomes an effort to find someone to blame or suggests that if we had never made any wrong choices in our lives, we might have lived forever. Church writes, "The hard truth is . . . we all die of something. Vegetarians die. Joggers die. Even people with low cholesterol die. . . .

However we may have lived, the ultimate culprit is not sin or squalor but life. Life draws death in its glorious train."

Next, he realizes that his death will be a source of anguish for his family and friends, and it is his obligation to be aware of that even if he won't be around to see it. He reaches out to them, articulating his fears so that they will feel free to express theirs, forgiving and seeking forgiveness. In that way, the loneliest thing any of us will ever do becomes just a bit less lonely.

And finally he draws comfort from his faith, not faith in a God of happy endings for good people and not faith in the certainty of a life in the hereafter but the faith that life is not meaningless just because it is not endless. "Everyone suffers but not everyone despairs. Despair is a consequence of suffering only when affliction cuts us off from others. The same suffering that leads one person to lose all hope can as easily promote empathy, a felt appreciation for other people's pain." It can also lead us to take pleasure in savoring one's time with loved ones, knowing it will be brief and therefore all the more precious.

Over the years, my appreciation of the books of Philip Roth has been enhanced by the realization that he and I are about the same age. I could identify with his characters, from the randy adolescents of *Goodbye, Columbus* and *Portnoy's Complaint* to the rueful middle-aged figure of Nathan Zuckerman.

When, in his most recent novels, I find heroes who are his (and my) age obsessed with the prospect of growing old and dying, I can't help feeling that this reflects issues with which Roth himself is grappling, and it saddens me that a writer of Roth's immense talent should be focusing on how little he has left rather than on how much. It bothers me because I recognize that same tendency in myself as I grow into my seventies and have to make allowances for physical and mental things I can no longer do as easily as I once did. It is the plaint of Ecclesiastes, who finds himself in old age thinking, I have striven to do so much and now I am running out of time and wondering what the point of it all was.

In contrast with this obsession with the gathering darkness, I am drawn to the attitude of the artist Marc Chagall, who just before his death at age ninety-seven completed his last painting entitled *Towards Another Light*, showing a young painter with wings (as if ready for flight) working at his easel and an angel descending from heaven to carry him off. I would like to see a person's last years (including my own) guided by the words of Spinoza that appear in the epigraph to this chapter, "A free man thinks of death least of all things, and his wisdom is a meditation of life, not of death."

The sin of Ecclesiastes—to focus too much on the fear of death, to see it as canceling out everything you have done in your lifetime—gives death more power than it deserves. Death is not the final word. Your life is the story; death is only punctuation. We sin against life and against everything that is holy and valuable in life if we let the fear of death rob us of our freedom to enjoy as much life as we are granted.

I read Roth's novel *Everyman* shortly after it was published, not realizing at the time that Roth had taken the title from a well-known medieval morality play and modeled his leading character after the hero of the play, a man who is terrified at the prospect of dying and dismayed to learn that neither friends nor family nor worldly success can postpone his passage. Happily, there is evidence that many people do deal with growing old and approaching the end of life more like Chagall than like Roth's protagonists. After Roth's novel appeared, two social scientists wrote to *The New York Times Book Review* citing the results of their research on middle-class Americans in their seventies. They wrote, "Only a small minority 'worry about oblivion.' Most accept their lives, including illness, loss and their many past misdeeds, and purposefully engage with the present. . . . Some despair, but they tend to be the same people who were also despairing in young and middle adulthood. . . . We share this note lest too many aging Americans take permission from Roth to dwell in the past and fear the future rather than seize the present."

My own experience endorses theirs. People are living longer, and most of them are no longer spending their last years watching television in an empty apartment and waiting for the end. More and more of them are finding useful, creative things to do, mentoring young people, organizing book clubs, and keeping themselves vital as they do so.

I have two specific suggestions for those people (and I include myself in their number) who realize that the years behind significantly outnumber the years ahead, and for those who may find themselves looking forward to death because they find their current lives unsatisfying. We have to cleanse our souls of accumulated bitterness, envy, and resentment. We have to get over our anger at people who may have hurt, cheated, or betrayed us, most of whom may be long dead themselves or long gone from our lives. I would say to people, Why do you insist on carrying that heavy baggage into whatever is waiting for you? Why are you giving those people such power over you, to define you as a loser, a bitter, jealous person? Let go and travel light.

And second, we have to be able to focus on one or two

meaningful things in our lives that we can feel we did well. A life doesn't have to be remarkable to be meaningful. If you were not that successful in business, if you never earned a lot of money, you can focus on the fact that you lived and worked with integrity, that you were a good neighbor and earned the respect of your coworkers. If as a mother you are disappointed at the way your children turned out, you can still take pride in your ability to go on loving them and caring about them despite your disappointment. Love them because of who you want to be, not just because of who you want them to be. If you worry that no one cares about you now that you are old and failing, find times to surround yourself with friends and family to give you the message of how much they care and to celebrate with them what your life has been about. Many years ago, when I was a young rabbi preparing to officiate at my first funeral (and only the third one at which I had been present), an older colleague gave me a valuable piece of advice. He told me, "Every life is a unique story, one that has never happened before. Your task as a eulogizer is to find that unique dimension and build your eulogy around it, so that friends and family will have that to remember."

When Thornton Wilder wrote his novel in an effort to make sense of the death of innocent people, he had them die when a bridge collapsed. Why did he have them die that way? Why not in a fire, an automobile accident, a plague, or at the hands of a violent murderer? Wilder may have been using the image of the fragile rope bridge over a chasm as a symbol of the precariousness of all of our lives. Whether we understand the bridge as carrying us to a better world or just taking us to tomorrow's problems and possibilities, each of us every day is making his or her way across a shaky bridge, aware that something might happen to us at any moment but at the same time realizing that if all we can think about is the fear of falling, we will never get anywhere in our lives. Feel the fear but cross the bridge anyway.

Toward the end of the eighteenth century, one of the dominant personalities in the world of Eastern European Hasidic Judaism was a man named Rabbi Nachman of Bratzlav. He enchanted his followers with his enigmatic stories and sayings, many of which are pored over to this day by theologians and psychiatrists alike. One of his many sayings became a popular song in Israel several years ago at a particularly tense time in Israeli society. This whole world, he said, is nothing but a narrow bridge, and for those who would cross it, the most important thing is not to be afraid.

We too, the only creatures who live with the daily awareness of our mortality, may feel that we are called on to cross that narrow bridge every day of our lives. If we let ourselves be paralyzed by the fear of falling into the chasm, we will never get anywhere or achieve anything. It will be the fear of death, not the fact of death, that will rob our lives of meaning. For us, as for Rabbi Nachman's disciples, the most important thing to remember is not to be afraid.

9

Conquering Fear

HOPE AND COURAGE ARE THE WILL OF GOD

> Without courage, we cannot practice any other virtue
> with consistency.
>
> MAYA ANGELOU

Yom Kippur, the Day of Atonement, is the most solemn
day of the Jewish year. It has been described as standing
at the intersection of life and death, of hope and fear. It is a day
to articulate our most heartfelt hopes for the coming year and
at the same time to acknowledge our deepest fears as to what
may be lurking in our future. "Who shall live and who shall
die, who shall flourish and who shall prosper, who by fire and
who by drowning?"

In the Jewish tradition, we prepare for the Day of Atonement by adding a psalm to the daily morning and evening service, a psalm that is recited at no other time of the year. For
forty days before Yom Kippur and for ten days afterward, we
recite the Twenty-seventh Psalm. It begins,

> The Lord is my light and my salvation; whom shall I fear?
> The Lord is the strength of my life; of what shall I be
> afraid? . . .

Though a host encamp against me, my heart will have
  no fear.

(PSALM 27:1, 3)

The message of the liturgy at this portentous time is, Yes,
the coming year may have its share of pain and problems, but
don't be afraid. You have the resources within you and around
you to cope with them. Don't let the fear of the unknown rob
you of the pleasure of anticipating all the good things that
await you.

When the psalmist tells us three times in the first three
verses of his psalm that he is not afraid, the message I hear is
that he *is* afraid, but he is working at mastering his fears. It is
like when your young child tells you, "I'm not afraid of big
dogs anymore." He is really saying that they still frighten him,
but he is working on his fears rather than giving in to them or
hiding from them. And where does the psalmist get the courage
to stand up against enemies and other dangers? It comes from
his faith in God, not a God who protects him from all trouble
and danger but a God who stands with him in time of trouble
and danger so that he never has to feel he is facing his problems alone. To the psalmist, God is the source of light,
strength, and salvation.

Sometimes God comes to the aid of fearful people by giving
them light. The light can come in the form of information:
"This will only hurt for a few seconds, and then you'll feel
fine." "We have done everything possible to make this a safe
and comfortable trip." "We have never had any problems with
this."

Or the light can be a bit of good news, a person reaching out
to us, fortune smiling on us in some unexpected way.

But what if experience has taught a person that the world is not always safe? That is when for us, as for the author of the Twenty-seventh Psalm, we find God in the sudden influx of strength we often feel as we confront the things that frighten us. We say to ourselves, I'm not sure I can do this. And God whispers to us, Yes, you can, because you don't have to do it alone. I will be with you; other people will be with you to help you through.

A woman listens to her oncologist describing the intimidating plan of treatment for her malignancy, and her first thought is, I'm not sure I can handle that. I don't know if I want to go through it. The doctor reassures her, Yes, you can. You're stronger than you think. And you won't be going through it alone. You have a supportive family. You have friends. You will have people here, doctors, nurses, chaplains, to help you do it. I'll connect you to a support group of women going through what you are going through, and you'll help each other. You can do it. And in most cases, she will.

I have seen it happen countless times. I have seen congregants asked to deal with misfortunes that they did not believe they were strong enough to survive, men and women who said to me through their tears, "I don't see myself ever getting over this." But from some source beyond themselves, a source none of us can explain or identify but one that I like to think of as God giving strength to those people who desperately need strength, people find emotional resources within themselves that they were sure were not there until the day they needed them, and then miraculously they appear.

An alcoholic attending his first meeting of a twelve-step program is skeptical as to how much it can help him. He says, I've tried to quit so many times. I promised my wife, I promised my kids, I promised my priest, and I sincerely meant it every time. But every time, I went back to drinking. Why will this be any different? His sponsor says to him, It will be different because this time you're not trying to do it alone, just you against the bottle. You'll be supported by people who know what the struggle is like because they have gone through it themselves. And, most important, you'll be turning to your Higher Power, however you understand that term, to give you the strength you need and have never had before.

I have lost track of how many people I have met in my travels who told me that the most profound religious experience they ever had came not in the church sanctuary on Sunday morning but in the church basement when they went to their twelve-step program on Tuesday night. That was when and where they felt the love and strength of God flowing into them. That was when they felt the truth of the words of the psalmist, "The Lord is the strength of my life; of what shall I be afraid?"

Finally, the author of the Twenty-seventh Psalm turns to God for salvation, to rescue him from enemies and danger. In the Hebrew Bible, "salvation" is less a theological term and more a practical one than it would become in later scripture. It is more like being saved from drowning than being saved from eternal damnation. Salvation is God's promise that, even when things are not going well, you may still survive and even flourish.

Picture a young man preparing for his first day on a new job, a job that represents the first step up a career ladder that he has been dreaming of ascending since he was an adolescent. The night before he has to report for work, he cannot sleep. He is afraid that he will not be up to the challenge. How does God ease his fears? God says to him, Of course you are fearful. You are about to step into the unknown, and the unknown is always dark and scary. But picture it this way: You are headed down a long road, a road that represents your career, and you don't know where it will lead. At the end of the road, there will be two doors. One will be marked Success, the other one Forgiveness and Resilience. One of those doors will open for you, but you won't know which one until you get there. But does it really matter which one? If you are talented and work hard, you may succeed or you may be victimized by bad luck or other people's meanness. If you are lucky, circumstances will guide you to succeed beyond your talents. Success would be very pleasant, but the alternative to success is not failure. The alternative to success is discovering that people don't love you for what you achieve; they love you for who you are. And the by-product of not succeeding in this job is the opportunity to pick yourself up and begin again.

In my theology, God's promise of salvation for people whose lives don't turn out as they hoped they would is not the promise of a better life in some world to come. It is the promise of forgiveness and a fresh start in this world. "Save me" need not only mean "Get me out of this situation." It may mean "Help me cope with this situation so that I am not destroyed by it."

I try very hard not to be judgmental about other people's religious beliefs that I may not share. My attitude is captured in the title of a book written by a colleague, Rabbi Brad Hirschfield, *You Don't Have to Be Wrong for Me to Be Right.*

The only expression of religion that I have trouble regarding with respect is one that pictures God as an ogre, watching over us to catch us in a large or small sin and to punish us severely for it. If there is one phrase I would like to see banished from theological discourse, it is the four words "the fear of God." I don't think much of a religion that tries to control its adherents by frightening them. I consider sermons that focus on hellfire and punishment to be remnants of an obsolete mind-set, the religious equivalents of alchemy and some of the bizarre theories of medieval medical malpractice. I don't believe God wants us to behave in certain ways because we are afraid of Him, any more than I would want my children or grandchildren to live upright lives because they are afraid of my catching them doing wrong and punishing them. I believe God wants us to do right and good things because we have come to understand that they are right and good. Obedience for obedience's sake out of fear of punishment is the morality of pets and little children. A God who uses fear and threats to control people's behavior, or a clergyman who does it in God's name, is like a parent or teacher who uses fear and threats to control children. It's something you do as a last resort because nothing else works.

Where the phrase "the fear of God" occurs in the Bible, I don't believe it refers to being afraid of God. I take it to refer to the sense of awe that overwhelms us when we contemplate the greatness and majesty of God. Fear makes a person feel small, vulnerable, eager to run away and hide. Awe expands the soul and makes us want to draw closer. To lean out of a tenth-floor window is to feel fear. To lean over for a better look at the Grand Canyon is to experience awe.

I believe that God wants us to be in awe of Him and of His values. I believe that God wants us to be in awe of His power, greater than the power of any human being or assembly of human beings. But I do not believe that God wants us to be afraid of Him. Fear casts out love as surely as love casts out fear.

After God's experience with Adam, who disappointed God not so much by eating the forbidden fruit as by making his first words to God "I was afraid," God remains unsatisfied with the human race for twenty generations, until the time of Abraham, who, when told by God "the challenge will be great but don't be afraid," bravely takes his family and marches into the unknown. As I read that story, Abraham was able to do what God asked of him because he saw God as encouraging and accompanying him, unlike Adam, who saw God as standing opposite him to judge him. I have known too many people who think of themselves as deeply religious but whose life is defined by a constant unrelenting fear that they may have done something wrong, said something wrong, eaten something wrong and offended God in the process. I cannot believe that God wants His creatures to live like that.

A 2007 article in the science section of *Newsweek* magazine reported the findings of scientists that "people's sense of emotional security shapes whether they become altruistic or selfish, tolerant or xenophobic, open or defensive." The person who has come to see the world as a safe and friendly place is likely to be more charitable to others, in both the financial and emotional sense of the word. The person who feels secure in another's love will feel freer to share his love with the less fortunate. Volunteers who were asked to meditate for several moments on someone who loved and cared for them, a parent, a friend, a lover, or God, were "more willing to give blood and do volunteer work, and less hostile to ethnic groups other than their own." To me, that is what religion is supposed to be about.

I believe that hope and courage, not fear and timorous obedience, are the will of God. Courage is not the absence of fear; it is the overcoming of fear. Courage is looking fear in the face and refusing to be intimidated. Courage is the firefighter rushing into a burning building or the soldier going into battle, fully aware of the dangers they are facing but accepting the challenge to do what duty calls on them to do for something they believe in. Courage is the young mother crippled in an accident or diagnosed with a degenerative disease who continues to raise her children and tend to her household instead of dissolving into self-pity. Viktor Frankl treated his patients who were paralyzed by fear by telling them, "Go out and do what you are afraid of. Expect the worst to happen." He would tell the agoraphobics, people who have a fear of being in public places, to get out of the house and go to the most crowded market they could find. He would tell patients with a fear of heights to climb a ladder. When they did it and the worst did not happen, he would say to them, "There, that wasn't so bad, was it?" Similarly, the Sufi poet Rumi challenged his readers to welcome their fears and sorrows, "meet them at the door laughing and invite them in." And some seven hundred years after Rumi, Rabbi James Jacobson-Maisels expressed a similar thought in these words: "When the fear arises, rather than shrinking back from it, ignoring it or violently overcoming it, one just tries to relax into it. . . . Fear, accepted and embraced, is no longer fear but at most a realistic concern with some future event. . . . In embracing fear, anger, desire or other 'unwanted' emotions, a certain space is created, a space created by the shock of non-opposition."

When I was a boy growing up in Brooklyn, one of the men I admired most was a young Manhattan rabbi named Milton Steinberg. He was everything you could ask a rabbi to be, brilliant, eloquent, a compassionate pastor with a tenderness that may have been shaped in part by his own fragile health. I was deeply saddened by his death in his midforties. In the course of my own studies for the rabbinate, I acquired all of his books, several of them published posthumously. He has an essay in one of his books to which I have often returned over the years. It is entitled "The Fear of Life."

We are all too familiar with the fear of death. But Steinberg suggested, in his book *A Believing Jew*, that there is a parallel fear of life. Only human beings are afraid of life, because only human beings can imagine the future. He wrote, "We fear for our children because we know what strange paths they may wander. We are timorous about our health because we can picture ourselves in the grip of malignant disease." And we are afraid of the future because it may lead to failure, hardship, and pain. Because we yearn for so much, life can disappoint us in so many ways. Because there are people in our world whom we care about, life can hurt us. How can we get over our fear of life?

Steinberg's first recommendation is that we face reality without illusions. Life may feel more pleasant, the future may seem more hopeful, if we deny reality, but no one can live courageously if his life is based on pretense and denial. I have read accounts of people who would tell friends that they were bank officers when they were in fact bank tellers because they found the truth embarrassing. I have heard of people who, when they lost their jobs, would continue to get dressed for work in the morning, leave the house, and spend the entire day reading newspapers at Starbucks because they were embarrassed to tell anyone that they had been fired. I have dealt with congregants who refused to go to a doctor to discuss their symptoms, telling themselves that there couldn't be anything seriously wrong with them because they were good people and did not deserve it. I have counseled men and women who stubbornly refused to notice evidence that their mates were seeking affection outside of the marriage, closing their eyes to a problem at a time when it might still have been possible to solve it, because the truth was too painful for them to acknowledge. They lacked the courage to look at their lives honestly, but reality cannot be denied forever.

Steinberg uses the term "disillusioned" to describe the outlook he would urge us to have. We usually think of "disillusioned" as describing someone who has given up his hopes and ideals. But for Steinberg "disillusioned" means having the courage to face life as it really is, without illusions. Face your problems and deal with them rather than hide from them, and you will discover that you are stronger than you think.

The second ingredient in Steinberg's prescription for curing us of the fear of life is a sense of duty. Do what you have to do even if it scares you. Eleanor Roosevelt once wrote, "You gain strength, courage, and confidence by every experience in which you stop to look fear in the face [and] you are able to say to yourself, 'I lived through this horror. I can take the next thing that comes along.' . . . You must do the thing you think you cannot do." Steinberg puts it this way: "Let the mother tend her young and let the poet sing his song, and the laborer dig his ditch and the merchant do his best. And if life is hard and the child grows into an ungrateful [adult] and the poet's song falls on deaf ears, if the laborer digs his ditch in vain and the merchant fails in his business endeavors, then at least each will have done his or her duty."

Steinberg's third step in meeting fear with courage is rooted in the realization that we don't have to do it alone. One of my favorite aphorisms comes from a nineteenth-century Hassidic rabbi who once said, "Human beings are God's language." When we call out to God in our distress, God answers us by sending us people. Any path is easier to travel when you have somebody's hand to hold.

Sociologists studying the religions of primitive societies concluded that the earliest forms of religion evolved not so much to connect people to God as to connect them to other people. When there was a death, when there was war or famine, when there was a natural disaster, religion brought people together, much as people filled their churches and synagogues on the weekend after 9/11. They just needed not to be alone. That is why a colleague of mine has suggested that the true test of the effectiveness of a church or synagogue is not the size or beauty of its building or the attendance at services but how well people come through for each other in difficult times and how generously they share their happiness with each other in good times.

And finally, there is the resource of faith, not the belief that God is a Santa Claus figure who will give us what we want if we have been good, not the illusion that all stories have happy endings, but the stubborn conviction that we are strong enough to survive misfortune, rejection, and failure. My faith teaches me that no good deed is ever wasted, that in some way, perhaps at another time, perhaps in another place, the world becomes a better, cleaner, braver place because of what I do.

Where do I turn when the world scares me, when I fear for my well-being, for my family, for my neighborhood, for my country, for the survival of our planet? Where do I find the will to offer further sacrifices on the altar of doing the right thing? I summon up memories of the past, times when I had to do something I wasn't sure I would be able to do and somehow found myself capable of doing it and doing it well, from embarking on a career in the rabbinate without any assurance that I would be good at it to helping raise a child with an incurable illness. I think of times I faced the challenge of doing something that I believed was the right thing to do. When I acted on my best instincts, sometimes it worked out well and sometimes it didn't. But when I look back on those occasions when I was afraid to do what I knew was right, I do so with regret and a measure of embarrassment. I find the courage to do the right thing now by calling up memories of how good it felt when I did what I thought was right and how weak and embarrassed I was when I let the fear prevail. I don't enjoy failure any more than the average man does, but I feel better about having tried and failed than I do about times when I was afraid to try.

I confront my fears with the knowledge that failure and rejection are not fatal, that the people who love me love me for who I am and for what I stand for at my best, not for what

I achieve. And I keep reminding myself that hope and courage are the will of God. I leave you with the words of the philosopher-psychologist William James. "These, then, are my last words to you: Be not afraid of life. Believe that life *is* worth living and your belief will help create the fact."

LIVING A LIFE THAT MATTERS

Most of us need to feel that we matter in some way; perhaps this explains the high value placed on titles, corner offices, and even fleeting celebrity. But most of us also need to feel that we are good people. In this luminous yet practical book of spiritual advice, Harold Kushner bridges the gap between these seemingly irreconcilable needs, showing us how even our smallest daily actions can become stepping stones toward integrity. Drawing on the stories of his own congregants, on literature, current events and, above all, on the Biblical story of Jacob, the worldly trickster who evolves into a man of God—Kushner addresses some of the most persistent dilemmas of the human condition: Why do decent people so often violate their moral standards? How can we pursue justice without giving in to the lure of revenge? How can we turn our relationships with family and friends into genuine sources of meaning?

Inspiration/978-0-385-72094-6

THE LORD IS MY SHEPHERD

Rabbi Kushner believes that the Twenty-third Psalm—perhaps the most cherished chapter of the Bible—offers spiritual riches that can change a person's life. He has found that these simple, beautiful verses have an almost magical power to comfort and calm. The psalm does not pretend that life is easy, but it offers a masterful guide to living in the world with faith and courage. Drawing on over forty years of his own thinking, on other biblical scholars, and on history, Kushner demonstrates how this sustaining work can help us cope with almost any aspect of life, from mundane jealousies to the death of a loved one to unimaginable tragedies of global proportions.

Inspiration/978-1-4000-3335-5

With his signature warmth, Harold S. Kushner turns to the experience of Moses to find the requisite lessons of strength and faith—fundamental lessons that teach us how to overcome the disappointments and frustrations that life inherently brings. From the examples of remarkable resilience and humanity that Moses provides, we can learn how to weather the disillusionment of dreams unfulfilled, the pain of a lost job or promotion, a child's failures, divorce or abandonment, and illness. We learn how to meet all disappointments with faith in ourselves and the future, and how to respond to heartbreak with understanding rather than bitterness and despair—how to be our best selves even when things don't turn out as we had hoped.

Inspiration/978-1-4000-3336-2

WHEN BAD THINGS HAPPEN TO GOOD PEOPLE

When Harold Kushner's three-year-old son was diagnosed with a degenerative disease that meant the boy would only live until his early teens, he was faced with one of life's most difficult questions: Why, God? Years later, Rabbi Kushner wrote this straightforward, elegant contemplation of the doubts and fears that arise when tragedy strikes. Kushner shares his wisdom as a rabbi, a parent, a reader, and a human being. Often imitated but never superseded, *When Bad Things Happen to Good People* is a classic that offers clear thinking and consolation in times of sorrow.

Inspiration/978-1-4000-3472-7

ANCHOR BOOKS
Available at your local bookstore, or visit
www.randomhouse.com